Property of Covenant

GOD'S HEART...
OUR HOPE

God's Message for Man's Journey

Robert Palmer

Copyright © 2012 Robert Palmer.
All rights reserved. No part of this book may be used or reproduced by any means, graphic, electronic, or mechanical, including photocopying, recording, taping or by any information storage retrieval system without the written permission of the publisher except in the case of brief quotations embodied in critical articles and reviews.

The Robert Palmer portrait is by Adams Portrait Gallery, Commerce, MI.
ralphadamsphoto@yahoo.com

Scripture quotations are from the ESV Bible® (The Holy Bible, English Standard Version®), copyright © 2001 by Crossway Bibles, a publishing ministry of Good News Publishers. Used by permission. All rights reserved.

ISBN: 978-1-4497-3745-0 (e)
ISBN: 978-1-4497-3746-7 (sc)
ISBN: 978-1-4497-3747-4 (hc)

Library of Congress Control Number: 2012900824

Design by Erik Peterson & www.projecto3.com

WestBow Press books may be ordered through booksellers or by contacting:
WestBow Press
A Division of Thomas Nelson
1663 Liberty Drive
Bloomington, IN 47403
www.westbowpress.com
1-(866) 928-1240

Because of the dynamic nature of the Internet, any web addresses or links contained in this book may have changed since publication and may no longer be valid. The views expressed in this work are solely those of the author and do not necessarily reflect the views of the publisher, and the publisher hereby disclaims any responsibility for them.

Certain stock imagery © Thinkstock.
Any people depicted in stock imagery provided by Thinkstock are models, and such images are being used for illustrative purposes only.

Printed in the United States of America
WestBow Press rev. date: 1/18/2012

What People Say

"*God's Heart... Our Hope.* The title says it all. I found such joy in reacquainting with the fundamental truths of the faith and even some new ways of seeing how these truths fit together. Written for the lay person, the language is understandable, making the understanding of these doctrines easier to perceive and so to embrace."

Jan Adams, Homemaker

"For the new Christian or those who have drifted away from the faith, this is a must read. Dr. Palmer lays out in an easy to read style, a compelling rationale for being saved through faith. He reinforces the scriptural promise that our Lord will not desert us, but will be there for those prepared to go the distance with their belief in Him."

Basil Anderson, Former Executive for Campbell Soups & Staples

"A clear and concise apologetic of Biblical faith explained without the theological ostentatiousness that weighs down similar works. I found it uplifting and straightforward and should be a 'go to' reference book in any serious library. I highly recommend it."

Richard S. Barone, CLU, Planning Partners Financial Group

"I found this book to be an outstanding daily devotional. Its depth and thought provoking energy is a great way to start my day!"

Dave Berg, Retired Executive, Munsingwear

"I love this book! Put forth with such excellence and clarity. It is a real life changer! Having been a Christian over forty years, it is the Biblical truths in layman's terms that are expressed here that are revolutionizing my life. This is doctrinal truth at its best. *God's Heart... Our Hope* is where I want to live. I will study it again and again."

Carol Bleich, Educator

"I read this manuscript with great pleasure. It is very well written... a fine piece of work that truly honors our God of love... Thank you for writing it."

Barbara Carole, Author, Former Associate Editor, The Paris Review

"There is a bright and shining thought early in this book that excites. 'Knowledge of the heart of God and the ways of God powers hope that is steadfast and sure.' *God's Heart... Our Hope* is revealing and reliable. The reader will know the heart of God better than ever before. There is a masterful assembly of Scripture here that brings us closer to the throne."

Hal Green, Vice President, NBC News (retired)

"A comprehensive yet relaxed walk through the important aspects of the Christian faith written in a way that can be read through from front to back or used as a ready reference tool for the subject of interest. The writing is particularly targeted to the lay person with a wealth of Scriptural references... a book well worth having in your library and on your nightstand."

John Hunter, Retired Executive, Monsanto & Solutia

"*God's Heart... Our Hope* is both thought provoking and inspirational. The author's insights are supported by Scripture and appropriate."

Jim Lindsay, President, Lindsay Real Estate Company

"An impressive and readable explanation of Scripture's doctrines of grace. The chapter on God's covenant with His people is especially strong. May God bless this work."

Ralph Lund, Retired Executive, Chem Lawn Services Corporation

"This book lays out the doctrinal basis for our hope and faith in the unchartered, turbulent waters of our current age... The writing is superb! The author has one of the most eloquent, clear styles of any author I have ever read. The writing is so very tight. He does not waste a word and is never redundant."

Diane Lustig, Former Writer/ Analyst, C.I.A.

I have recently had the pleasure of reading Robert Palmer's book, *God's Heart... Our Hope*. This book is revolutionary in simplicity, and has opened my eyes to new and delightful ways to look at both the heart of God and the Word of God. The author's writing is compelling and opens the spiritual eyes of the reader to the true and tangible love of our Creator. I highly recommend this wonderful book to all who are searching for a deeper and clearer understanding of the benevolence of our loving Father.

Tamra Nashman, Author, Lecturer

"*God's Heart... Our Hope* is a must read that belongs in every Christian home. This is not just a 'read.' It is seminary education for those of us unable to attend seminary. I particularly found the chapters on 'effectual calling' and 'perseverance' clearly defined for the lay person."

Dr. Thomas C. Scott, Physician

"This book will be a blessing to many. The subject arrangement, flow and literary style is most readable. I pray that many will read its pages and be drawn closer to the Lord."

David Winscott, Ph.D., President, Winscott Investment Strategies

Dedication

This book is lovingly dedicated to my wife, Gloria.
With immense devotion she has skillfully shepherded
every chapter to its final form.

"Many women do noble things but you
surpass them all." †Proverbs 31:29

With equal delight this publication is dedicated
to my three daughters who have blessed their Mom & Dad
in numerous ways. To Kimberly Swedlund,
Michelle Beltz, and Janice Rood:

"You are our letter, written on our hearts,
known and read by all." †II Corinthians 3:2

"They devoted themselves to the apostles' teaching...
Awe came upon every soul...
And the Lord added to their number day by day
those who were being saved." †Acts 2:42-47

Table of Contents

Acknowledgements — xii

Introduction — 15

Chapter 1
Don't Land Without The Lights — 21

Chapter 2
Emptying An Ocean — 35

Chapter 3
Declare God's Majesty — 48

Chapter 4
Talk Of God's Glory — 60

Chapter 5
Our Humpty Dumpty Dilemma — 74

Chapter 6
Life Is Never Que, Sera Sera' — 87

Chapter 7
God's Finger On Man's Shoulder — 102

Chapter 8
Doing As We Please — 130

Chapter 9
One Call That Changes All — 144

Chapter 10
A Declaration Of Dependence — 155

Chapter 11
Going The Distance — 169

Chapter 12
Marathons Are Not For Wimps — 182

Quotes — 199

Acknowledgements

A SPECIAL WORD OF APPRECIATION to the Elders of Covenant Church, Naples for their support in the publication and promotion of this book by their Pastor-at-Large. In addition, a heartfelt word of thanks to Dr. Robert Petterson, Sr. Pastor of Covenant Church, and longtime friend. His discerning commentary has been of great value; his words of encouragement contagious.

Navigating the potential pitfalls and procedures of publishing is a task that has fallen to Hal Green, an esteemed elder and fervent friend. Without his determination and hard work this book never would have begun. With unyielding zeal, he has prodded me not to relent in this project. With equal determination, he has pursued the many agendas relating to publication.

In addition, the editorial input of Diane Lustig and John Hunter has been of immense help in navigating through the challenges of effectively communicating to God's people in the pew.

Most especially, this volume never would have seen the light of day were it not for the untold hours that were relentlessly, lovingly, and enthusiastically invested by my wife, Gloria.

Finally, with respect to the content of this publication, I make no claim to originality. Of course, for any writer, originality is most likely out of the question.

Rather, what has been attempted is an effort to express timeless Scriptural truths within a format that the average lay person would find easy to understand.

I have attempted to accomplish what Eric Hoffer describes this way: "Originality manifests itself most strikingly in what we do with what we did not originate."

Thus, I gladly express appreciation to the following publications that have contributed substantially to the thoughts expressed in *God's Heart... Our Hope*.

- *A Systematic Theology of the Christian Faith*
  Robert L. Reymond
- *Bitesize Theology*
  Peter Jeffery
- *Essential Truths of the Christian Faith*
  R.C. Sproul
- *God As He Longs for You to See Him*
  Chip Ingram
- *The Attributes of God*
  Arthur W. Pink
- *The Divine Inspiration of the Bible*
  Arthur W. Pink
- *The Knowledge of the Holy*
  A. W. Tozer
- *The Sovereignty of God*
  James Montgomery Boice
- *The Westminster Shorter Catechism* (A Commentary)
  G. I. Williamson
- *The Wonder of It All*
  Bryan Chapell
- *Truths We Confess* (3 volumes)
  R.C. Sproul

May God in His grace be pleased to use this volume to fortify His people with the kind of renewed hope that finds its source in a better understanding of their God as He has revealed himself on the pages of His Word.

INTRODUCTION

"There is nothing more important to the success of our journey
to a future we cannot control than that we keep hope alive."

QUOTES #1

WHAT FUELS THE CHRISTIAN'S HOPE for that journey he cannot control is a confidence that, "all the paths of the Lord are steadfast love and faithfulness for those who keep His covenant and His testimonies... Steadfast love and faithfulness spring up from the ground and righteousness looks down from the sky" (Psalm 25:10; 85:11). Crushing cares may abound, but a never-failing hope also abounds. It is a confident hope anchored in the reality that, "The Lord takes pleasure in those who hope in His steadfast love." (Psalm 147:11).

> *The believer's hope is a rational expectation that is measured, corrected, and enlarged by reference to the Word of God.*

This hope of God's covenant people is not an illusion. It is not a fanciful tilting at windmills. "I wait for the Lord, and in His Word I hope" (Psalm 130:5).

The believer's hope is a rational expectation that is measured, corrected, and enlarged by reference to the Word of God. It is courage nurtured by the knowledge of that "faith once for all delivered to the saints" (Jude 3). It is certainty nourished by a deep appreciation for biblical doctrine: A confidence supported by familiarity with sound biblical theology.

The Heart of God

In the classic comic strip "Peanuts," two of Charles Schultz's favorite characters are looking out the window at a steady downpour of rain. Lucy turns to her friend Linus and says, "Boy! Look at it rain." Being a bit fearful she then adds, "What if it floods the whole world." With an obvious child-like certainty, Linus responds, "It will never do that. In the ninth chapter of Genesis, God promised Noah that would never happen and the sign of the promise is the rainbow."

You can almost hear the sigh of relief in Lucy's voice as she tells her young friend, "Linus, you have taken a great load off my mind." Puffed-up with a feeling of great satisfaction and pride, Linus then pompously proclaims, "Sound theology has a way of doing that!"

We smile at the child-like certitude of the little guy, but he is right. Sound theology does take a load off our minds. It does so because of the kind of attention to Scripture that infuses a sense of peace-giving perspective into the lives of God's saints.

Knowledge of the heart of God and the ways of God powers the kind of hope that is steadfast and sure. "Knowledge of the Holy One is insight" (Proverbs 9:10).

> Knowledge of the heart of God and the ways of God powers the kind of hope that is steadfast and sure.

"There is," writes A. W. Tozer, "scarcely an error in doctrine or a failure in applying Christian ethics that cannot be traced to imperfect and ignoble thoughts of God." (Quotes #2) Why is that? It is because every teaching of the Bible originates in the heart of God, is an expression of the character of God, and increases the believer's hope in God.

So what is it that marks the heart of God? It is this: The Bible pictures a heart of perfect justice and transcendent righteousness. All of God's works "...are truth and His ways just" (Daniel 4:37). "I will proclaim the name of the Lord," writes Moses. "Ascribe greatness to our God!... His work is perfect, for all His ways are just. A God of faithfulness and without iniquity, just and upright is He" (Deuteronomy 32:3, 4).

God's people have every reason to be comforted and encouraged, knowing also that the heart of the Redeemer is characterized by a consummate wisdom that is infinite and faultless. "How unsearchable are His judgments and His ways past finding out" (Romans 11:33-34). "My thoughts are not your thoughts, nor are your ways my ways, says the Lord" (Isaiah 55:8-9).

Furthermore, every redeemed child of God reaps great and eternal benefit, knowing that the heart of their heavenly Father is gracious, passionate, and merciful. "Blessed is the one you choose and bring near to dwell in your courts... You, Lord, are good and ready to forgive and abundant in mercy to all those who call upon you" (Psalm 65:4; 86:5).

> *Every redeemed child of God reaps great and eternal benefit, knowing that the heart of their heavenly Father is gracious, compassionate and merciful.*

When reflecting on the sovereign justice and refreshing compassion of God, God's chosen people experience a renewing peace. This peace guards their thoughts and minds in Christ Jesus (Philippians 4:7). There is a sense of substantial certainty, knowing that their God has vowed, "I know the plans I have for you... plans for wholeness and not for evil, to give you a future and a hope" (Jeremiah 29:11). Charles Spurgeon writes, "I know nothing which can so comfort the soul; so calm the swelling billows of sorrow and grief; so speak peace to the winds of trial, as a devout musing upon the subject of the Godhead."

> Stayed upon Jehovah
> > Hearts are fully blessed
> Finding as He promised
> > Perfect peace and rest.
>
> —**Frances R. Havergal**

For every believer, El Shaddai is a safe harbor of hope. When fatigued, God becomes their rock in a weary land. When fearful, He becomes their high tower of safety and security. Nothing happens by chance. Their God upholds, guides, and governs all circumstances. He "works out everything in conformity with the purpose of his will" (Ephesians 1:11).

Little Linus gave voice to a wisdom greater than he knew. Sound theology does so much more than "take a load off our

INTRODUCTION

mind." A sound theology clarifies the ways in which the sovereign compassionate heart of God engages the sinful hurting heart of man. It is possible to give lip service to such a sound theology, yet fail to live a God-honoring life. But what is not possible is this: to live a consistently God-honoring life without also embracing a sound, biblical theology.

> *Theology clarifies the ways in which the sovereign compassionate heart of God engages the sinful hurting heart of man.*

The pages you are about to read attempt to set forth in a brief, clear, and accurate manner a number of fundamental Bible truths describing both the heart of God and the condition of man. These teachings of God's Word make that journey to a future we cannot control, one of unwavering hope, traveling with the God of all hope.

FOOD FOR THOUGHT

"We are to preach Christ in the fullness of His being and grace. We are to hold nothing back which God has revealed... The Holy Spirit will bless such faithful teaching. He will use the doctrines of His Word to convict and convert those destined for salvation. God saves through theology." QUOTES #3

CHAPTER 1

DON'T LAND WITHOUT THE LIGHTS

"If I were the devil, one of my first aims would be to stop folks from digging into the Bible… At all costs I should want to keep them from using their minds in a disciplined way to get the measure of its message." QUOTES #4

Christianity Is a Revealed Religion

So shall my word be that goes out from my mouth; it shall not return to me empty, but it shall accomplish that which I purpose, and shall succeed in the thing for which I sent it. †Isaiah 55:11

Your word is a lamp to my feet and a light to my path. †Psalm 119:105

But be doers of the word, and not hearers only deceiving yourselves. †James 1:22

LOOKING OUT THE WINDOW OF an airport terminal at night is a captivating experience. The many multi-colored lights stretching up and down the runways are fascinating. My friend John Denard, a commercial pilot, assures me that those numerous lights are indispensable to aviation safety. They help insure that the pilot is able to navigate a safe take off and landing. John also tells me that there are a number of different lighting systems. For example, *Approach Light Systems* are primarily intended to provide a means to transition from instrument flight to visual flight for landing. The *Runway Identifier Lights* provide rapid and positive identification of the approaching end of a runway. Then there are the *Runway Edge Lights* whose obvious purpose is to outline the edges of runways at night or during low visibility conditions.

God assures His people, they will not trip in the darkness, provided they do not stray from Scripture.

Similarly, the Psalmist reminds God's people that there is in life a most critical and essential set of "guiding lights." It is God's Word. God assures His people, they will not trip in the darkness, provided they do not stray from Scripture.

General Revelation is Given to All People

For the wrath of God is revealed from heaven against all ungodliness and unrighteousness of men, who by their unrighteousness suppress the truth. For his invisible attributes, namely his eternal power and divine nature, have been clearly perceived, ever since the creation of the world, in the things that have been made. So they are without excuse. †**Romans 1:18-20**

FOR THOSE WHO HAVE NO attachment to the Bible, God has a message: They are not excused for what they believe or for how they behave. How come? The answer is in the message of Romans 1: What can be vividly seen in the majesty of creation communicates a message that is transparent. It is not concealed! Nature shouts God's glory.

> God, all nature sings Thy glory,
>   And Thy works proclaim Thy might;
> Ordered vastness in the heavens,
>   Ordered course of day and night;
> Beauty in the changing seasons,
>   Beauty in the stormy sea;
> All the changing moods of nature
>   Praise the changeless Trinity.
> —David Clowney

Yet, in spite of what can be seen in the grandeur, complexity, and beauty of creation, stubborn man remains determined to suppress the message that confronts him. By way of illustration, Dr. Carl Sagan, a brilliant astronomer and author, is a man impacted by the incredible complexity that he observes in the design of the world all around him. When he describes the intricacy of a human chromosome, he writes:

> A single human chromosome contains twenty billion bits of information. How much information is twenty billion bits? What would be its equivalent, if it were written down in an ordinary printed book in modern human language? Twenty billion bits are the equivalent of about three billion letters. If there are approximately six letters in an average word, the information content of a human chromosome corresponds to about five hundred million words. If there are about three hundred words on an ordinary page of printed type, this corresponds to about ten million pages. If a typical book contains 500 pages, the information content of a single human chromosome corresponds to some 4,000 volumes.

Obviously Dr. Sagan understands far more than most about the complexity of creation. Yet, he also professes to have no belief in God, and therefore no attachment to the Bible. Instead, he transfers what ought to be an unmistakable sense of God's majesty to unworthy objects. What this man of science observes is simply attributed to impersonal forces that operate throughout the cosmos. To him, the grandeur and complexity of all that is around has nothing to do with the supernatural Creator of the heavens and earth.

God inwardly reveals his law through the human conscience.

The message of Romans 1 is a stinging rebuke of such unremitting unbelief. "Although they knew God, they did not honor him as God, or give thanks to him, but they became futile in their thinking and their foolish hearts were darkened" (Romans 1:21). What the apostle writes not only highlights what can be seen in the glory of creation, it also affirms that

God inwardly reveals His law through the human conscience. It is for this reason John Calvin writes, "We are all born with a sense of the divine." God's creatures know right from wrong. They do not need to be somehow taught. Yet once more, says Romans 1, natural man is quite capable of suppressing this instinctive sense of right and wrong.

Man does this because there is within the human psyche a powerful and sinful self-centeredness There is an unfounded pride that drives mankind to quench his awareness of right and wrong. The creature's conscience is powerful. It tugs at those sins within, yet almost instinctively, man seeks to suppress it.

Centuries ago in the ancient capital of Thailand, there was an ingenious device that, like man's conscience, revealed the presence of imminent danger. The object functioned in a way that is similar to present-day electronic devices at the airport.

The gateway leading into the king's palace was made of lodestone, a natural magnet. If a would-be assassin came in through the opening with a concealed dagger, the lodestone would pull at the hidden weapon like an invisible hand. Sensing danger, the guilty guest would impulsively move toward the weapon. Trained guards, watching every response, would then grab the criminal. And man's conscience is a force that acts in a similar fashion. It tugs at concealed sins.

> There is an unfounded pride that drives mankind to quench his awareness of right and wrong.

There is, therefore, says Romans 1, this general revelation God has given to all mankind. It takes the form of creation and conscience. At the same time, such disclosure cannot make plain God's plan of salvation. To gain a saving knowledge requires special revelation.

Special Revelation in the Incarnation of Jesus

Long ago, at many times and in many ways, God spoke to our fathers by the prophets, but in these last days he has spoken to us by his son, whom he appointed the heir of all things, through whom also he created the world. He is the radiance of the glory of God and the exact imprint of his nature, and he upholds the universe by the word of his power. †**Hebrews 1:1-3**

Let the word of Christ dwell in you richly, teaching and admonishing one another in all wisdom. †**Colossians 3:16**

....

THE ZENITH OF SUCH "SPECIAL revelation" is the incarnation of the Son of God. Jesus is the one who is both Author and Finisher of man's salvation. In His coming mankind has seen God's glory. It is the "...glory as of the only son of the Father, full of grace and truth" (John 1:16). The apostle says, "...He pitched his tent among us." In doing so, all mankind has beheld the benevolent covenant making and covenant keeping character of the God of all grace.

The incarnation of Jesus is a revelation that is qualitatively superior to what had come long ago through the prophets, says the writer of Hebrews. How come? It is because God's ancient prophets were simply servants in the house of God. But Jesus is very different: He is God's incarnate Son, "...whom He appointed the heir of all things, through whom also He created the world" (Hebrews 1:2)

For this reason, when the Son speaks it is as one whose revelation is final. He is "...the radiance of the glory of God" (Hebrews 1:3). He is the wisdom of God personified. Man will not escape the condemnation of God if he refuses to listen to this one who is "...the eternal Word of God." "See that you do not refuse Him who is speaking," says Hebrews 12:28. How come?

Because He alone is the one who has laid that firm foundation upon which the Christian's hope of eternal life is built.

> What more can He say
> Than to you He hath said,
> To you who for refuge
> To Jesus have fled.
> —Rippon's "Selection of Hymns" (1787)

Special Revelation in the Canon of Scripture

All Scripture is breathed out by God and profitable for teaching, for reproof, for correction, and for training in righteousness, that the man of God may be competent, equipped for every good work.
✝ II Timothy 32:16-17

For no prophecy was ever produced by the will of men, but men spoke from God as they were carried along by the Holy Spirit.
✝ II Peter 1:21

BECAUSE CHRISTIANITY IS A REVEALED system of belief, when the Son of God came to earth, He also acknowledged, "Man shall not live by bread alone, but by every word that proceeds from the mouth of God" (Matthew 4:4). The Savior was saying that what the prophets wrote is a message from God. It is sufficient. It contains everything necessary for salvation. For abundant life. For eternal life.

The writings of the New Testament, when added to those of the Old Testament, provide that definitive statement of "The faith that was once for all delivered to the saints" (Jude 3). They are the very writings that clarify how God "...has caused us to be born again to a living hope, through the resurrection of Jesus Christ from the dead to an inheritance that is imperishable, undefiled, and unfading, kept in heaven for you" (I Peter 1:3).

When the apostle Paul describes such special revelation, he speaks of the fact that, "All Scripture is given by inspiration of God" (II Timothy 3:16). Just as men expel breath when they speak, so the apostle was saying, God was "breathing out" His message through the writings of His prophets and apostles. For this reason, the writings of these men are an authoritative message. It also is why Jesus announced, "Scripture cannot be broken" (Matthew 4:4).

The sixty six books of the Bible are to be embraced as "the norm." They are "the measuring rod." It is why they are also referred to as the canon of Scripture. These are the inspired writings that have consistently communicated the intrinsic authority of God's prophets and apostles.

In seeking to determine which books command such authority, God's people for centuries have considered the following to be required "marks of canonicity." First, a given book must have apostolic endorsement. Second, the writing must have been received as authoritative by the early first and second century church. Third, the message communicated must be in harmony with other writings of the prophets and apostles, about which there never has been doubt.

> *The sixty-six books of the Bible are to be embraced as "the norm". They are "the measuring rod".*

Sixteen hundred years have passed since the church, following the above "marks of canonicity," resolved all issues relating to the authoritative nature of each of the sixty six books of our present-day Bible. In that entire time, never has there been a serious attempt made to add to or take away from any of these sixty six books. Consistently, these sixty six books communicate with an intrinsic apostolic authority.

Authenticity of the Bible

THERE IS IMPRESSIVE EVIDENCE POINTING to the fact that the Bible is what it claims to be! The evidence is both external and internal. It speaks with commanding authority. For example, by any measurement, the following internal evidence cannot be minimized.

Internal Evidence

THE SIXTY SIX BOOKS OF the Bible were written over fifteen hundred years by forty nine different authors, speaking three different languages. These forty nine authors lived in different geographic locations, involving very different cultures, and yet, never do these writings contradict one another.

Additional internal evidence comes from the fact, that in one archaeological discovery after another, objective observers have been impressed by the historical accuracy of the Bible. For example, the renowned archaeologist William F. Albright has written, "Discovery after discovery has established the accuracy of the innumerable details and has brought increased recognition to the value of the Bible as a source of history."

> *The impressive number of fulfilled prophecies throughout the Biblical record serves as irrefutable internal evidence to the authenticity of the Scriptures.*

There are also the impressive number of fulfilled prophecies throughout the Biblical record that serve as irrefutable internal evidence to the authenticity of the Scriptures. For example, seven hundred and fifty years before the birth of Jesus, the prophet Micah wrote that the Christ child would be born in the obscure village of Bethlehem. The prophet Zechariah, six hundred years before Calvary, revealed that Jesus the Messiah would be betrayed for thirty pieces of silver. The prophet Isaiah, seven hundred and twenty years before the crucifixion of Jesus, wrote that Messiah would be put to death with thieves. After his death, this same prophet wrote, Messiah would be buried in a rich man's tomb.

There is an inherent quality of Scripture demonstrating that it is unique from other literary documents.

Such prophecies relating to the coming of the Christ are numerous, and they have been fulfilled, just as they were foretold centuries earlier. It truly is an amazing dimension of internal evidence.

Authorities in the mathematical discipline of statistical probability have estimated the likelihood of the myriad of biblical prophecies being fulfilled is greater than one in a trillion. No wonder Peter would later write: "...we have the *Prophetic Word* made more sure, to which you do well to pay attention as a lamp shining in a dark place" (II Peter 1:19).

External Evidence

THE TESTIMONY IS EQUALLY IMPRESSIVE in regard to external evidence. There is an inherent quality of Scripture demonstrating that it is unique from other literary documents. C. S. Lewis, Cambridge University Professor and The Chair of Medieval and of Renaissance English Literature, affirmed that he could not read the Bible without recognizing the transcendent quality of what he read. There is in Scripture an exceptional quality, wrote Lewis, a quality he found missing from other literature.

Similarly, consider the remarkable power residing in the Bible. Every year, it is a power that changes untold millions of lives. The nineteenth century British pastor, C. H. Spurgeon, knew what he was talking about when he wrote, "There is no need for you to defend a lion when he is being attacked. All you need to do is open the gate and let him out."

From Genesis to Revelation, there is no confusion. No ambiguity. No contradiction. All sixty six books contain one harmonious, life-transforming message of divine origin. Together, they make up the believer's "...only infallible rule of faith and practice."

If Christians are to know the heart of God and experience the hope of God, they must diligently study the Word of God. "Your word is a lamp to my feet and a light to my path ...Your testimonies are my heritage forever, for they are the joy of my heart" (Psalm 119:105;111).

> *If Christians are to know the heart of God and experience the hope of God, they must diligently study the Word of God.*

> Holy words long preserved
>> For our walk in this world;
> They resound with God's own heart
>> O let the ancient words impart.
> Words of life, words of hope
>> Give us strength help us cope;
> In this world wher-e'er we roam
>> Ancient words will guide us home.
> —Lynn deShazo

Christian, don't land without the lights!

FOOD FOR THOUGHT

"Christianity is the religion of a book. Christianity is based upon the impregnable rock of Holy Scripture. The starting point of all doctrinal discussion must be the Bible. Upon the foundation of the Divine inspiration of the Bible stands or falls the entire edifice of Christian truth… Surrender the dogma of verbal inspiration and you are left like a rudderless ship on a stormy sea—at the mercy of every wind that blows. Deny that the Bible is without any qualification, the very Word of God, and you are left without any ultimate standard of measurement and without any supreme authority." QUOTES #5

QUESTIONS FOR FEEDBACK

1. What does revelation through Scripture do for us that revelation in creation does not do?

2. What does unregenerate man do when given the truth about God? How does God respond?

3. By what standards does the Bible teach that God will judge people in the final judgment?

4. In II Peter 1:21, why does the apostle defend the authority and inspiration of the prophets?

5. What evidences can you give that the Bible is the inspired, authoritative Word of God?

6. What do you think is meant by the statement that Scripture must be self-interpreted?

CHAPTER 2

EMPTYING AN OCEAN

"The Trinity means that God is one in one respect, namely in substance... when the church confesses that the living God is a Triune God, it is saying that the one life substance, Deity, exists consciously as three persons... If God were not triune, Jesus Christ could not be God... The Christian could never really celebrate Christmas, for there would be no real incarnation (God in the flesh). If God were not triune the Holy Spirit would not be God and what would then happen to the strengthening and abiding presence of God in our lives? Indeed, the biblical teaching of the Trinity is no luxury for a few 'deep thinkers' who love to juggle words. It is the keystone of the whole building of Christian truth." **QUOTES #6**

ST. AUGUSTINE, ONE OF THE greatest minds in Christendom, in seeking to describe Trinitarian deity, commented that the God of the Bible is "...an infinite circle, whose center is everywhere and whose circumference is nowhere."

One day as this man walked along the shore of the Mediterranean Sea, he saw a young boy aggressively digging in the sand. "What are you trying to do?" Augustine asked. Looking up, the boy naively replied, "I want to empty the sea into this hole that I'm digging."

A childish response? Of course! But it made an impact on the Bishop of Hippo. Here's why. For seemingly endless hours this renowned scholar of the church had been wrestling with the complex concept of the Trinity. Although exhausted, he remained unable to adequately explain the mystery.

> *The greatness of God truly is far beyond the capacity of man to comprehend.*

Repeatedly, the little boy's words resonated within, "I want to empty the sea into this hole I'm digging." It was precisely this kind of hopeless exercise that also had been engaging this brilliant theologian. Augustine later wrote that he thought to himself, "Am I not trying to do the same thing as this child, seeking to exhaust with my reason, the infinity of God—trying to collect the infinity of God, within the limits of my own mind?"

The greatness of God truly is far beyond the capacity of man to comprehend. "If you try to understand the Trinity, you will lose your mind," wrote Wilbur Smith. "But if you deny the Trinity, you will lose your soul." However, this much we can do: We can present the biblical evidence on which the doctrine of Trinity rests; we can highlight our difficulty in grasping God's perspective on the concept of "personhood;" and we can seek to appreciate the Scriptural evidence relating to how this doctrine of God's Trinitarian Being impacts man's salvation.

Biblical Evidence On Which the Doctrine of the Trinity Rests

The Lord said, 'Behold, man has become like one of us. †**Genesis 3:22**

The Lord said, 'Come, let us go down and confuse their language. †**Genesis 11:7**

I and the Father are one... †**John 10:22-39**

Jesus is the image of the invisible God... In him all the fullness of God was pleased to dwell. †**Colossians 1:15-20**

...Why has Satan filled your heart to lie to the Holy Spirit? You have not lied to me (Peter) but to God. †**Acts 5:3-4**

The grace of the Lord Jesus Christ and the love of God and the communion of the Holy Spirit be with you all. †**II Corinthians 13:14**

TO BEGIN WITH, THE TERM "trinity" never is mentioned in the Bible. However, it is equally true that the concept of "trinity" is repeatedly underscored throughout the Scriptures.

The New Testament writers saw no contradiction between Christianity's Trinitarian God and Judaism's Monotheistic God. There is a reason why this is so. The apostles were quite familiar with passages such as Isaiah 6:8: "I heard the voice of the Lord saying: 'whom shall I send, and who will go for us?'" Also, they were familiar with how, in speaking of the coming Messiah, Isaiah had written, "Now the sovereign Lord has sent me, *with his spirit*" (Isaiah 48:16).

> *The concept of "trinity" is repeatedly underscored throughout the Scriptures.*

These men were familiar with how Zechariah, in speaking of the anticipated appearing of Messiah, excitedly wrote: "Sing aloud, O daughter of Zion... Rejoice and exult with all your heart... the Lord your God is in your midst, a mighty one who will save..." (Zechariah 3:14,17).

The apostles were familiar with how the prophet Malachi wrote, "The Lord whom you seek will suddenly come to his people; and the messenger of the covenant in whom you delight, behold, he is coming, says the Lord of hosts" (Malachi 3:1). Because the apostles knew these prophecies, they never stumbled over the Trinitarian nature of the monotheistic God of Israel.

There is further biblical evidence of God's Trinitarian Being in the New Testament baptismal formula announced by Jesus. Those wishing to be identified as "the followers of Jesus" are to be baptized " ...in *the name* of the Father and of the Son and of the Holy Spirit." They are not to be baptized in *"the names"* of the Father, Son, and Holy Spirit Why? Because the baptismal formula is not pointing to three *separate beings*. Rather, Jesus is pointing to one monotheistic, yet Trinitarian God.

Neither does Jesus say, "...baptizing them into *the* name of the Father, Son, and Holy Spirit." If Jesus had used the definite article "the" only once, in effect, He would be saying that the Father, Son, and Holy Spirit are simply three *modes of one person*.

In John 10:22-39, the fact that Christians are utterly secure is a truth grounded in the reality that, "I and the Father are one," says Jesus. The first and second person of the Trinity are equal in authority, and equal in power. Both Jesus and the Father also are to be identified as objects of man's faith.

It is a theme repeated throughout the New Testament. In Romans 9:5, Jesus is described as "*...over all, God blessed forever.*" In Titus 2:13, He is described as "*...our great God and Savior.*" In Colossians 1:15-20, He is "*The image of the invisible God.*" Jesus is the one in whom "*...all the fullness of God was pleased to dwell.*" In I Timothy 1:17 He is described as "*...immortal, invisible, the only God.*"

What is true of Jesus, is equally true of the Holy Spirit. In Acts 5:3-4, Peter confronts Ananias, "...why has Satan filled your heart to lie to the Holy Spirit?... You have not lied to me, but to God." In II Corinthians 13:14, within the apostle's benediction, are all three Persons of the Trinity: "The grace of the Lord Jesus Christ, and the love of God and the communion of the Holy Spirit be with you all." In I Peter 1:2, followers of Jesus are described as those who are the "...elect according to the foreknowledge of God the Father, in sanctification of the Holy Spirit and for obedience and sprinkling of the blood of Christ."

It is the Holy Spirit who inspires the Scriptures. He convicts the world of sin, righteousness, and justice. He empowers believers to boldness, love, and self discipline. He intercedes for believers. The Holy Spirit also raises believers from the dead to glory.

> *Fully grasping the glory and greatness of the infinite God of Scripture is beyond the capacity of man's finite mind.*

Does God's infinite triune being remain a complex mystery to finite minds? Absolutely! But that does not mean Trinitarian Monotheism is simply a "contradiction in arithmetic." Rather, it underscores the truth that fully grasping the glory and greatness of the infinite God of Scripture is beyond the capacity of man's finite mind.

God's Concept of "Personhood" Is Different From Man's

Jacob was left alone. And a man wrestled with him until the breaking of day... Your name shall no longer be Jacob but Israel, for you have striven with God. †**Genesis 32:24-30**

Behold, the virgin shall conceive and bear a son, and you shall call his name Immanuel (God with us) ...For to us a child is born, to us a son is given... and his name shall be called... Mighty God, Everlasting Father... †**Isaiah 7:14; 9:6**

...If I do not go away, the Helper will not come but if I go, I will send him to you. †**John 16:7**

TO A GREAT EXTENT MAN'S difficulty has much to do with the fact that the Creator's concept of "personhood" is very different from the creature's understanding.

Such a reality should come as no great surprise! Why? Because there are other abstract concepts such as "time" in which God's reckoning is very different from man's. God's finite creatures measure time in minutes, hours, and days. Not so the Creator! "Do not overlook this one fact," writes the apostle Peter, "that with the Lord one day is as a thousand years, and a thousand years as one day" (II Peter 3:8). Finite creatures clearly have a concept of time that is quite different from the Creator's way of envisioning time. Measuring time, for the Creator, is not a matter of minutes, hours, and days. It is merely the possibility of the sequence of events.

> *There is nothing in human experience that can compare with the biblical description of God in His Trinitarian Form*

Augustine recognized this difference between God's reckoning and man's seeking to understand the Biblical teaching of Trinity. He conceded that man has a problem that in many ways truly is insurmountable. The problem is this: There is nothing in human experience that can compare with the biblical description of God in His Trinitarian form.

The creature is left with what God chooses to reveal about Himself in the Bible. It therefore is a dilemma demanding *faith*.

That should come as no great surprise! Looking at God's created solar system also is beyond man's capacity to understand. The incredible vastness of creation demands faith. In many dimensions of life, faith is the only bridge over the chasm between man's limited understanding and the wonder of who God is. Such faith simply makes things *possible*. It does not make things *easy*!

In terms of Trinitarian Monotheism, man also has a need to better understand the word *"person."* What does this term "*person*" signify? What does it represent? What does it symbolize? To begin with, the noun "*person*" is derived from the compound Latin word "*persona.*"

The prefix "*per*" means "through." The root "*sono*" means "to speak." To a great extent, therefore, when believers speak about "*persons*" in the Trinity, they are at least partially saying that the God of the Bible "*speaks*" through each of these Beings within the Godhead.

R. C. Sproul, in Volume 1 of Truths We Confess provides a helpful illustration of this complex concept of "*persona.*" In the Broadway play J.B., when Basil Rathbone, seeks to assume the role of God, he holds before his face a mask that symbolically depicts God. The actor then speaks through this mask, or "*persona*," supposedly representing God.

The actor then changes gears. He seeks to take on the role of Satan responding to God. At this juncture he holds before his face a second mask, that is obviously intended to symbolize or to picture the "*persona*" of Satan. The actor proceeds to speak through this second mask, this second "*persona.*"

The critical point is this: each mask represents a different "*persona.*" Yet, the voice behind the two masks is the solitary voice of just one person. At least to some degree, Basil Rathbone, in that Broadway play was dramatizing our dilemma, as we seek somehow to fathom the meaning of the Latin word "*persona.*"

> *In many dimensions of life, faith is the only bridge over the chasm between man's understanding and the wonder of who God is. Such faith simply makes things possible. It does not make things easy.*

Do we continue to stagger and stammer, stymied in our finite ability to comprehend the infinite "*person-hood*" of God? Of course! Even a superior intellect such as John Calvin was compelled to write, "If the church were to discover another word that more accurately conveyed the intention of Scripture, I would welcome it."

A major dimension of our struggle is that we also are seeking to understand that which is *"spirit."* When the Westminster Shorter Catechism says, "God is a spirit, infinite, eternal and unchanging," it is pointing to the fact that God's nature is removed from all association with familiar materialistic things in man's experience.

> *A major dimension of our struggle is that we are also seeking to understand that which is "spirit".*

It is saying, God is invisible. He is unlike any created being. He is infinite. He is omnipresent. Therefore the three persons of the one Godhead all are omnipresent. They never exist independently of each other, and it is this vital dimension of the Godhead that has *everything* to do with man's salvation.

The Trinity and Man's Salvation

My father, if it be possible, let this cup pass from me; nevertheless not as I will, but as you will. †Matthew 26:39

For God did not send his son into the world to condemn the world, but in order that the world might be saved through him. †John 3:17

If the spirit of him who raised Jesus from the dead dwells in you, he... will also give life to your mortal bodies through his spirit who dwells in you. †Romans 8:11

BECAUSE FATHER, SON, AND HOLY SPIRIT share in the same *omnipresence* and *omniscience,* they also share in what they know each will do to accomplish man's salvation. Each not only has full objective knowledge of what the other will do; each also has his own subjective and specific role to fulfill.

The Father and the Holy Spirit objectively know that it is the Son *alone* who will take upon himself the sins of His people. It is the Son *alone* who will bear the penalty of their sins in his own body on the cross. It is the Son alone who will transfer to them his perfect obedience, his perfect righteousness.

The Father and the Holy Spirit certainly know in an objective way, that this is the Son's assignment. But it is the Son *alone* who subjectively knows that He and He alone will be the one to be crucified on Golgotha's hill. He *alone* will experience "God forsakenness" for the sins of God's chosen people.

> *Because Father, Son, and Holy Spirit share in the same omnipresence and omniscience, they also share in what they know each will do to accomplish man's salvation.*

Because all three persons share in the same omnipresence and omniscience, both the Son and the Holy Spirit know in an objective way that the Father *alone* will justify those chosen from before the foundation of the world. Both the Son and the Holy Spirit know in an objective way that it is the Father *alone* who will establish the grounds upon which man's salvation will be based.

At the same time, however, it is the Father *alone* who subjectively knows that He *alone* will be the one to justify those described as His "chosen generation," His "holy nation," His "royal priesthood." Neither the Son nor the Holy Spirit ever subjectively thought it would also be *their* role to accomplish this mission.

What also is true is this: both the Father and the Son objectively know it was the Holy Spirit's mission *alone* to quicken and regenerate spiritually dead sinners. They knew it is the Holy Spirit's subjective mission, and His mission *alone* to effectually call sinners to the Savior.

Together all three "Personae" are infinite in their omniscience. Each person of the Godhead also has a clearly defined subjective mission they alone will accomplish. The three "Personae" do not act *independently*. Rather, they function as One *omniscient* "being," accomplishing man's salvation.

> *If this magnificent mystery is disregarded... we condemn ourselves to a state of being that is blinded to the glory and grandeur of God's saving grace through Christ Jesus His Son.*

Bottom line, it comes to this: If God is not both *triune* and also *monotheistic* in His *omniscient* "being," then the Father has no grounds for adoption. The Son is incapable of paying the "ransom price" for the sinners' adoption; and the Holy Spirit cannot quicken spiritually dead sinners, making them to be "new creatures in Christ Jesus."

Trinitarian Monotheism obviously remains a complex puzzling problem for our finite minds to fully comprehend. But, if this magnificent mystery is disregarded, in the words of J. I. Packer: "...We sentence ourselves to stumble and blunder through life blindfolded." We condemn ourselves to a state of being that is blinded to the glory and the grandeur of God's saving grace through Christ Jesus His Son.

FOOD FOR THOUGHT

"Sometimes it is thought that Christianity teaches the absurd notion that 1 + 1 + 1 = 1. That is clearly a false equation. The term Trinity describes a relationship not of three gods, but of one God who is three persons. Trinity does not mean… that there are three beings who together are God. The word Trinity is used in an effort to define the fullness of the Godhead both in terms of His unity and diversity." QUOTES #7

"We are deeply conscious that the Trinity is a mystery beyond our comprehension. The glory of God is incomprehensible. There are no analogies… There is no way we can picture this truth." QUOTES #8

QUESTIONS FOR FEEDBACK

1. If the word "person" does not help in our thinking about the Trinity, why do we use it?

2. According to I Corinthians 2:14, who is it that cannot understand the things of God, and why?

3. Considering the problems being faced by the church at Corinth, how would Paul's Trinitarian benediction in II Corinthians 13:14 be appropriate?

4. How would you demonstrate that the God revealed in the Old Testament is the Triune God?

5. Why do you believe the apostles had no difficulty embracing teaching relative to the Trinity?

6. As you think about the work of each person of the Trinity, would it be possible for a sinner to be saved, if one aspect were missing?

EMPTYING AN OCEAN

CHAPTER 3

DECLARE GOD'S MAJESTY

"What comes to our minds when we think about God is the most important thing about us... All of God's acts are consistent with all his attributes. No attribute contradicts any other, but all harmonize and blend into each other in the infinite abyss of the Godhead... God being who he is cannot cease to be what he is"

QUOTES #9

WHAT PEOPLE THINK ABOUT GOD will have a direct bearing on the ways in which they respond to God. Unfortunately, many tend to trivialize their Creator. They treat Him as some sort of benevolent benefactor who somehow makes things "come out right" in life. Such thinking is a whole lot more than inappropriate; it is insulting to the majesty of God.

God Is Infinite In His Perfection

Oh, the depth of the riches and wisdom and knowledge of God! How unsearchable are His judgments and how inscrutable His ways!... For through Him and to Him are all things. To Him be glory forever. Amen.
† Romans 11:33-35

GOD IS INFINITE IN HIS being. God is *self-sufficient*. There is within Him all that is excellent, all that is perfect, all that composes true happiness. It is why the apostle Paul writes, "Who has known the mind of the Lord or who has been his counselor? Or who has given a gift to him that he might be repaid?" (Romans 11:34-35). Recognizing God's self-sufficiency, the apostle John writes,

> *God is dependent on nothing outside of Himself.*

"Worthy are you, our Lord and God, to receive glory and honor and power, for you have created all things, and by your will they existed and were created" (Revelation 4:11).

We created beings require a whole lot of "something else." God requires *nothing*! God is dependent on nothing outside of himself. He is "...from everlasting to everlasting." Of equal and undeniable certainty is this: man never can fathom the infinite being of God with the "measuring stick" of his finite mind.

Immortal, invisible, God only wise,
   In light inaccessible hid from our eyes,
Most blessed, most glorious, the Ancient of Days,
   Almighty, victorious—Thy great name we praise
—Walter Chalmers Smith

God Is Incomprehensible

Can you find out the deep things of God? Can you find out the limit of the Almighty? It is 'higher than heaven'—what can you do?
† Job 11:8

THE BIBLE NEVER IMPLIES THAT God is completely unknown. He simply never can be perfectly known by finite man. Only the infinite can perfectly know the infinite. It is for this reason that Jesus said, "No one knows the Son except the Father, and no one knows the Father except the Son and anyone to whom the Son chooses to reveal him" (Matthew 11:27).

> *Only the infinite can perfectly know the infinite.*

When it is said, "God is incomprehensible," it does not mean God is "unreasonable." It does not mean God is "irrational." And it does not mean God is "absurd." Throughout history, brilliant minds always have stepped forward to defend the faith. Augustine, Calvin, C.S. Lewis, Francis Schaeffer and a host of others have followed in the footsteps of the apostle Paul, engaging those skeptics standing on "Mars Hill." All have recognized reason and logic as gifts of the Holy Spirit. All have delighted to use such gifts, taking pleasure in destroying "...arguments and every lofty opinion raised against the knowledge of God" (II Corinthians 10:15).

To say God is incomprehensible is simply to affirm that the finite cannot grasp the infinite. It cannot be done for an obvious reason. There is lacking in man an adequate "reference point." By way of partial illustration, a clock with a luminous dial can be seen in the dark because the dial glows in the dark. However, everything changes in the light of high noon. Suddenly, the luminous quality of the dial becomes concealed by the sunlight. The light that had been seen in the dark, becomes insignificant because it is exposed to the intensity of the sun.

> *The finite cannot grasp the infinite... There is lacking in man an adequate reference point.*

In a somewhat similar way, whatever man understands of the things of God, are the very things that will pale into insignificance in the "Shekinah" glory of God. "Shekinah" glory is dazzling. It is brilliant beyond comprehension. It therefore is a blinding light to finite man.

God Is Almighty

Oh, Lord God! It is you who has made the heavens and the earth by your great power and by your outstretched arm! Nothing is too hard for you. †**Jeremiah 32:17**

THE POWER WITHIN THE "MUSHROOM cloud" of an atomic bomb is a dreadful thing to contemplate. But atomic power pales in comparison to the almighty, creative power of God. To get a feel for the immensity of the universe created by Almighty God consider this: *alpha centauri* is the nearest star to our sun. It is about 4.3 light years away, or 25.3 trillion miles. And this is our *nearest* star!

> *Atomic power pales in comparison to the almighty, creative power of God.*

Andromeda is the nearest large galaxy to our *Milky Way* galaxy. It is 2.2 light years away! In other words, if a person were traveling 186,000 miles *per second* for 2.2 million years, that individual would reach the outer fringes of *Andromeda*. Once more, remember, this is the *nearest* galaxy to ours! And there are numerous galaxies in the universe.

How did this galaxy get there? God Almighty spoke it into existence. Such utterly unimaginable statistics ought to produce at least these three responses within all mankind: it should create a sense of respect for the almighty power of God; for the believer, it should bring about an even greater response. It should serve as a strong sense of comfort, knowing that, "If this God is for us, who can be against us?" (Romans 8:31). Whether individuals are believers or not, there ought to be a sense of deep humility in view of this almighty being, whose creative handiwork and glory is proclaimed in his works of creation.

Coming back to God's redeemed people, Scripture records a merciful message. It is meant to nurture and encourage God's "chosen ones." "The Lord your God is in your midst, a *mighty one* who will save; he will rejoice over you with gladness; he will quiet you by his love; he will exult over you with loud singing" (Zephaniah 3:17). With great confidence and joy the redeemed love to sing:

> Be still and know that I am God, O'er all exalted high;
> > The subject nations of the earth
> My name shall magnify
> > The Lord of Hosts is on our side, Our safety to secure;
> The God of Jacob is for us
> > A refuge strong and sure.
>
> —The Psalter, 1912 (from Psalm 46)

God Is Sovereign

Yours, O Lord, is the greatness, and the power, and the glory, and the victory, and the majesty, for all that is in the heavens and in the earth is yours. Yours is the kingdom, O Lord, and you are exalted as head over all. †I Chronicles 29:11

THE EXPRESSION, "SOVEREIGNTY OF GOD," once was generally understood. It frequently was a subject expounded by pastors from evangelical pulpits. That is not so much the case today.

For this reason, God speaks of "...foolish and senseless people, who have eyes, but see not, who have ears, but hear not" (Jeremiah 5:21).

When we refer to the "sovereignty of God," we are referring to the "supremacy of God." The kingship of God. God's sovereignty declares, God IS God. He is the Most High. "All inhabitants of the earth are accounted as nothing, and he does according to his will among the host of heaven and among the inhabitants of the earth" (Daniel 4:35).

God is omnipotent. He has all power. He is omniscient. He has all knowledge. He is omnipresent. He is in all places. It is because God is sovereign, that He also is free to do whatever He wills, anywhere He wills, at any time He wills and to carry out every detail of His will.

> *To say God is sovereign is to declare that nothing happens in life that God has either not allowed or decreed for the ultimate good of those He calls to be his chosen people.*

To say God is sovereign is to declare that nothing happens in life that God has either not allowed or decreed for the ultimate good of those He calls to be His chosen people.

> The Lord is King!
> Lift up thy voice
> O earth; and all ye heavens rejoice:
> From world to world the joy shall ring,
> "The Lord omnipotent is king!"

The Lord is King! Who then shall dare
Resist his will, distrust his care,
Or murmur at his wise decrees
Or doubt his royal promises?
—Josiah Conder

God Works All Things According to the Counsel of His Will

As for you, you meant evil against me, but God meant it for good, to bring it about that many people should be kept alive, as they are today. ✝ **Genesis 50:20**

And we know that in all things God works for the good of those who love Him have been who called according to His purpose. What then shall we say to these things? If God is for us, who can be against us? ✝ **Romans 8:28,31)**

GOD DOES NOT WORK THINGS out according to popular opinion. He works according to the Counsel of His unchangeable and righteous will.

Such truth ought to cause every believer's heart to rejoice! Why? Because, if it were not so, neither would they know the joy of sins forgiven.

In Gethsemane, the Savior knew in a perfect way, something that His followers all too frequently forget: God *always* will do, only what is best and what is righteous.

It is for this reason, that even while suffering indescribable agony, Jesus prayed, "...nevertheless, not my will but *yours* be done."

Wisdom would dictate this: what Jesus uttered in Gethsemane, should continually be preeminent in the believer's mind when he prays.

There is nothing the child of God can say that will cause God to alter His righteous will. For that matter, the child of God can speak nothing to the Father that he does not already know. God does not *need* man's counsel. God already knows every word uttered by man, before that word is even spoken.

The child of God does not pray in order to change God's mind. The believer's prayer is offered to change the limited mindset of a finite and dependent child of God. It is offered in order to bring this child into *communion* with the mind of the Heavenly Father, who loves to hear what is on his heart.

James has this in mind when he writes: "The prayer of a righteous person has great power as it is working" (James 5:16). He is teaching this: when the righteous believer brings petitions, two things are happening. They are considering who *they* are. And they also are considering who *God* is. They are acknowledging that God is the *only one* who is both *willing* and *able* to order all things in their life according to the counsel of *His* will.

Will God always answer the prayers of His children? Absolutely! But He will answer in only one way: according to *His* righteous wisdom. According to *His* perfect will. True wisdom is achieved when that child of God humbly accepts and is comforted by the fact that *God alone* knows both what is best to grant and what is best not to grant. It undeniably pleases God to do what needs to be done. It equally pleases a loving Heavenly

> There is nothing the child of God can say that will cause God to alter His righteous will.

> It is a great comfort to know that God takes all things in the lives of His children, even wicked things, and causes such painful predicaments to work according to HIS perfect will and HIS saving purpose.

Father not to do for His needy child what His perfect wisdom dictates should not be done.

It is this indisputable reality that stands behind the apostle Paul's words of assurance that "...God works *all things* according to the counsel of *His will*." Paul is saying, God's will is perfect. It is righteous. It therefore is unchangeable. And because this is true, what happens to the child of God comes about because this infinitely loved child is "...called according to *His purpose*."

It is a great comfort to know that God takes all things in the lives of His children, even wicked things, and causes such painful predicaments to work according to *His* perfect will and *His* saving purpose. It also is the reason why God promises, "I know the plans I have for you... plans for wholeness and not for evil, to give you a future and a hope" (Jeremiah 29:11). Such assurance also is why the believer can sing:

> Whate'er my God ordains is right:
>   Holy his will abideth;
> I will be still whate'er he doth,
>   And follow where he guideth.
> God is my God; though dark my road,
>   He holds me that I shall not fall:
> Wherefore to him I leave it all.
>
> —Samuel Rodigast

FOOD FOR THOUGHT

"A spiritual and saving knowledge of God, is the greatest need of every human creature… The foundation of all true knowledge of God must be a clear mental apprehension of his perfection as revealed in Holy Scripture. An unknown God can neither be trusted, served, nor worshipped." QUOTES #10

QUESTIONS FOR FEEDBACK

1. What false image of God do many people seem to embrace today?

2. When it is said that certain attributes of God are "incommunicable," what is meant?

3. Can you describe a common objection to God's absolute sovereignty?

4. In Revelation 4:1-11, what is it about the four living creatures that suggest the eternal power of God? What does this say about who God is and how he relates to his creation?

5. In I Corinthians 2:7-9, the apostle speaks of God's "secret wisdom." What is he referring to? What does he mean?

6. Looking at Ephesians 4:11, in what ways does Paul say the providence of God brings him such peace and contentment?

CHAPTER 4

TALK OF GOD'S GLORY

"The attributes of God are essential to the nature of God… It is precisely in the sum total of His attributes that His essence as God finds expression." **QUOTES #11**

ONCE MORE IT MUST BE affirmed that a faulty understanding of Biblical doctrine relating to who God is can be disastrous. It can be compared to a missile aimed just one degree off target. At first the difference does not appear to be that decisive or dangerous. But it won't be long before the dramatic consequences of that one degree are realized. The missile will totally miss its intended target.

Bad doctrine is a lot like that missile heading toward the wrong objective. At first bad doctrine may be seen as "no big deal." Folks may even say, "It's not that serious." But over time, the unintended effects of error tend to compound. Not infrequently bad doctrine becomes so entrenched and serious, it may not be corrected.

> Much like that missile aimed one degree off target, a faulty understanding of the character of God eventually will lead to unintended and ruinous consequences.

It is hard to imagine a biblical doctrine more important than what is taught about the attributes of God. Much like that missile aimed one degree off target, a faulty understanding of the character of God eventually will lead to unintended and ruinous consequences.

To begin with, there is a preeminent sense in which God's attributes are not so much about characteristics which He possesses. More accurately, God's attributes are *who He is*! He is "Immortal, invisible, God only wise, in light inaccessible hid from our eyes," says the hymn writer. He is unequaled. Unsearchable. Unchangeable. He is perfect. Righteous. Everlasting. He is just and true.

The Goodness of God

The Lord God is a sun and shield; the Lord gives grace and glory;
no good thing does he withhold from those who walk uprightly.
†Psalm 84:11

> Every good gift and every perfect gift is from above, coming down from the father of lights... †James 1:17

WHEN WE SPEAK OF GOD'S "goodness," we are referring to that quality in God that causes Him to *bless* His people. To *delight* in His people. The God who is our "sun and shield" takes pleasure both in the gifts He gives and in those who are the recipients of those gifts. God takes great satisfaction in the glad response of His people.

But what also is true is this: God does not respond to His people in the same way every time. Similarly, God does not respond every time the way in which His people would like him to respond. But God *does* respond. He responds because He desires his children to know that He is *good*. He responds because He desires that His children trust His provision.

God who "...gives grace and glory" always will be their Defender, Redeemer, and Friend.

It is why the apostle writes, "...for those who love God all things work together for good..." It is why he writes, "If God is for us, who can be against us? He who did not spare His own Son but gave Him up for us all, how will He not also with Him graciously give us all things?" (Romans 8:28, 31, 32).

It is this very saving purpose of God that guarantees "good" for His people. That does not mean life will always move according to our desires, or our prayers, or our expectations; yet God assures us that His providence always is working in ways we many times cannot see. Behind what we cannot see and cannot understand, God's providence is actively controlling whatever is happening to us.

Eventually God's providential "goodness" will bring about that which will accomplish our ultimate good and God's ultimate purpose. How do we know this? Paul answers: it is the supreme gift of God's Son for us that guarantees our good and God's glory. It is the very reason why the redeemed of the Lord can lift their voice and sing with assurance:

> Praise to the Lord who doth prosper
>   thy work and defend thee;
> Surely his goodness and mercy
>   here daily attend thee;
> Ponder anew what the Almighty will do,
>   If with his love he befriend thee.
>
> —Joachin Neander

The Mercy of God

Keep yourselves in the love of God, looking for the mercy of our Lord Jesus Christ unto eternal life. ✝Jude21

Not by works of righteousness which we have done, but according to his mercy he saved us, by the washing of regeneration, and renewing of the Holy Spirit. ✝Titus 3:5

MANY TIMES CHRISTIANS WILL POINT to the fact that grace gives what we do not deserve. Specifically, God's grace gives *eternal life*. Christians also will emphasize that God's mercy withholds what we deserve. Mercy withholds *eternal punishment*.

In reality, God's mercy goes much deeper. It is deeper because God's mercy reflects his *lovingkindness*. The Hebrew word for "mercy" appropriately can be translated as it is in Psalm 17:7: "Wondrously show your steadfast love (lovingkindness), O Savior of those who seek refuge from their adversaries at your right hand." The same thought is expressed in Psalm 36:7: "How precious is your steadfast love (lovingkindness), O God! The children of mankind take refuge in the shadow of your wings."

God's mercy is not simply the withholding of punishment. God demonstrates His mercy in the act of giving help, in having compassion on one who is afflicted. "Because your steadfast love (lovingkindness) is better than life," writes the Psalmist, "my lips will praise you" (Psalm 63:3).

God's mercy reflects His lovingkindness

This merciful lovingkindess is one of the most frequently mentioned themes of Scripture. When God appears to Moses, He declares His name as "...the Lord, a God merciful and gracious, slow to anger, and abounding in steadfast love and faithfulness" (Exodus 34:6). It is the Lord who led His people out of Egypt to their promised land. At every juncture of this journey God's liberated people become overwhelming debtors to the mercy of the Lord.

It is a mercy that is active, boundless, never failing. It is pure joy to undeserving hearts. Mercy is God's practical way of doing two things: making His people aware of their unworthiness and delivering them from their misery. This is preeminently seen, writes Jonathon Edwards, in the "...mercy of God, which he shows to a sinner when he brings him home to the Lord Jesus Christ." "Most certainly," says Edwards, "this is the greatest and most wonderful exhibition of mercy and love, of which men are ever the subjects."

Those who have embraced this saving mercy of the Lord have every reason to sing:

> Thy mercy, my God,
> > Is the theme of my song,
> The joy of my heart,
> > And the boast of my tongue;
> Thy free grace alone,
> > From the first to the last,
> Hath won my affections,
> > And bound my soul fast.

The Wisdom of God

With God are wisdom and might; he has counsel and understanding.
†Job 12:13

Great is our Lord... his understanding is beyond measure. †Psalm 142:5

My thoughts are not your thoughts, neither are your ways my ways declares the Lord. For as the heavens are higher than the earth, so are my ways and my thoughts than your thoughts. †Isaiah 55:8-9

Oh, the depth of the riches and wisdom and knowledge of God! How unsearchable are his judgments and how inscrutable his ways!
†Romans 11:33

THE TWENTIETH AND TWENTY FIRST Centuries have produced an information explosion unparalleled in human history. People have instant access to volumes of knowledge at the click of a "mouse." Yet, with all the information today's people can accumulate, their wisdom remains impotent to answer the most basic spiritual questions of life.

> With all the information today's people can accumulate, their wisdom remains impotent to answer the most basic spiritual questions of life.

Man has a wisdom that is able to benefit physical life. But that is where his wisdom ends. Because of man's unwillingness to submit to the wisdom of God's Word, man's mind is unable to discern the spiritual dimensions of life.

As a consequence, man has no power to change his heart. He has no understanding to satisfy or solve the dilemma of his soul.

In contrast, through the wisdom contained in His Word, God is able to bring about the best possible results, by the best possible means, and for the longest possible time. Again, quoting from A. W. Tozer's volume, *The Knowledge of the Holy*, "All God's acts are done in perfect wisdom... Not only could his acts not be better done; a better way to do them could not be imagined." QUOTES 12

The Holiness of God

There is none holy like the Lord... †I John 2:2

...Holy, holy, holy is the Lord of hosts, the whole earth is full of his glory! †Isaiah 6:3

....

PREEMINENTLY THE BIBLE SAYS GOD is holy. He is free from evil. He is absolute moral perfection.

God's holiness impacts everything else about God. God's love is a holy love. God's justice is a holy justice. God's mercy is a holy mercy. God's anger is a holy anger. God does nothing that is not perfect in holiness. Because this is true, whatever God does has no possibility of failing.

> This transcendent holiness of God does not conform to a standard. God's holiness is the standard.

No study could possibly be of more importance or value than the study of God's holiness. To be holy is to be utterly distinct and unique. It is to be spiritually pure. It is to be sacred and untainted by evil. "We know nothing like the divine holiness," writes A. W. Tozer, "the natural man is blind to God's holiness. He may fear God's power and admire his wisdom, but holiness, he cannot even imagine." QUOTES 13

This transcendent holiness of God does not conform to a standard. God's holiness is the standard. And in addition, it also affirms God is able to see clearly and completely into the soul of man. He sees all the "warts," all the wickedness.

When Isaiah cries out, "...Woe is me," it is because he realizes there is nothing good, or commendable, or righteous in him. In one of Charles Westley's hymns, he recognizes, that without such a convicting certainty of God's utter holiness and man's utter defilement, neither can there be a longed for sense of sins forgiven. An awareness of sins forgiven only can come through a prayerful recognition of the fact that: "Just and holy is thy name. I am all unrighteousness; False and full of sin I am; Thou art full of truth and grace."

The Justice of God

Clouds and thick darkness are all around him; righteousness and justice are the foundations of his throne. †Psalm 97:2

The Lord is righteous in all his ways, and kind in all his works.
†Psalm 145:17

You are of purer eyes than to see evil, and cannot look at wrong.
†Habakkuk 1:13

For the wrath of God is revealed from heaven against all ungodliness and unrighteousness of man, who by their unrighteousness suppress the truth. †Romans 1:18

THE CONCEPT OF JUSTICE ADDRESSES an uncompromising allegiance to an unwavering standard that punishes evil. Unfortunately, people do not always witness such a quality of justice in today's world.

Not too many years ago, the Supreme Court in Pennsylvania overturned the murder conviction of a man, because the prosecutor had read from the Bible in his closing remarks to the jurors. The newspaper account of this incident did not specify the passage of Scripture read. It simply stated, that in his closing argument, the prosecutor had read from the Bible. Many people read the report and understandably asked: Where is the justice in such a verdict?

God's justice is never like that. It is far more formidable than man's ever could be. Individuals always will get what they deserve from God. They will get what they deserve because,

"Righteousness and justice are the foundation of God's throne" (Psalm 97:2). His justice is not arbitrary. It is a revelation of His inmost nature. It is perfectly righteous. It is moral. It is both omniscient and omnipotent.

> The Lord, the everlasting King,
> > Is seated on His judgment throne;
> The righteous Judge of all the world
> > Will make His perfect justice known.
>
> —The Psalter, 1912 (Psalm 9)

The Love of God

Because your steadfast love is better than life, my lips will praise you. †Psalm 63:3

...God is love. In this the love of God was made manifest among us, that God sent his only Son into the world, so that we might live through him. In this is love, not that we loved God, but that he loved us and sent his Son to be the propitiation for our sins. †I John 4:7-10

GOD'S LOVE IS THE ONE attribute most praised by the vast majority of people. It also is an attribute often misunderstood. Why is this? It is because the affection of God is not patterned after human emotions. Man's love to others normally is extended because of something that is seen in that other person.

> *God's love confirms His very nature. It is a love that is infinite and unchanging. It is a love that transcends the grasp of man's mind.*

God's love is not like that! It is not a sentimental thing. It is free. It is spontaneous. It is undeserved. It is uncaused. It is unsought. It is unimaginable. The only reason God loves any of His creatures is to be found in His sovereign will. "It was not because you were more in number than any other people that the Lord set his love on you and chose you," wrote Moses of God's ancient people (Deuteronomy 7:7).

And what was true in Moses' day is no less true today. In any age, there is nothing in God's people that attracts His heart to them. On the contrary, there is in them "...no good thing," says Scripture. "In this is love... that he loved us," and sent his son to pay an awful price to redeem us.

God's love confirms His very nature. It is a love that is infinite and unchanging. It is a love that transcends the grasp of man's mind. It is a love before which unworthy sons and daughters can only bow in adoring worship.

The Faithfulness of God

The steadfast love of the Lord never ceases; his mercies never come to an end; they are new every morning; great is your faithfulness.
†Lamentations 3:22-24

UNFAITHFULNESS IS ONE OF THE saddest realities of life. In married life, infidelity abounds. In the business world a man's word is no longer his bond. Even in the church, those who at one time solemnly vowed to faithfully preach the Word, have become unfaithful to that Word.

> *The God of our salvation is utterly dependable.*

How refreshing to lift one's eyes above life's scenes of discouragement and ruin, to know the God of our salvation is utterly dependable. "The Lord your God is God, the faithful God who keeps covenant and steadfast love with those who love him" (Daniel 7:9). Faithfulness is an essential quality of the very being of God. Without faithfulness God would not be God. "If we are faithless, he remains faithful—for he cannot deny himself" (II Timothy 2:13).

Understanding God's unchanging faithfulness is something that goes far beyond the feeble, finite comprehension of man. "Your steadfast love, O Lord, extends to the heavens, your faithfulness to the clouds" writes the Psalmist (36:5). God never forgets. He never fails. He never falters in His steadfast loving commitment to His covenant people.

He is a God who makes good on every promise He has given. He does so, despite man's failings. He does so, for the sake of His covenant promise. He never will forsake His own.

"God is not a man, that he should change his mind. Has he said, and will he not do it? Or has he spoken, and will he not fulfill it?" (Numbers 23:18).

> *This certainly does not mean the believer always will understand the ways in which God is orchestrating the events of life.*

This certainly does not mean the believer always will understand the ways in which God is orchestrating the events of life. But what is certain is this: God never will let His sons and daughters down. Upon His faithfulness—upon the rock-solid guarantee of His word, rests their hope of future blessedness. Therefore, with absolute certainty the redeemed of the Lord lift up their voices and sing:

> Trembling soul, beset by fears
>   'Thy God reigneth.'
> Look above and dry thy tears,
>   'Thy God reigneth.'
> Though thy fears with power assail
>   Not against thee shall prevail.
> Trust in him—he'll never fail.
>   'Thy God reigneth.'
>   —Fred S. Shepherd

FOOD FOR THOUGHT

"What you think about God shapes your whole relationship with Him… Our relationships are formed by our perceptions of each other. How you see somebody makes all the difference in the world, as does how you think the other person sees you." QUOTES 14

QUESTIONS FOR FEEDBACK

1. How is God able to be both a God of love and forgiveness and also a God of justice who punishes sin?

2. What does it mean to call God holy? Why would this lead someone to worship God? Why does the Bible particularly emphasize this holiness of God?

3. How can a holy God get his "hands dirty," dealing with sinful humans?

4. In looking at Romans 9:25-29, in the Old Testament quotes that are cited by the Apostle Paul, what qualities of God stand out to you?

5. If God says he will not remember the sins of his redeemed people, does that mean God has a bad memory?

6. How would you describe the goodness of God?

TALK OF GOD'S GLORY

CHAPTER 5

OUR HUMPTY DUMPTY DILEMMA

"In the fall of mankind, something ghastly happened. The image of God was severely tarnished. Our ability to mirror his holiness has been greatly affected so that now the mirror is fogged. We cannot ask, 'When does the individual become a sinner?' for the truth is that human beings come into existence in a state of sinfulness. They are seen by God as sinful because of their solidarity with Adam." **QUOTES 15**

AT THE BASE OF THE Tetons in Wyoming lies Lake Jackson. At times, early in the morning when the lake is perfectly calm, the reflection of those mountains is magnificently mirrored on the lake's surface. But if a person were to take one little flat stone and skip it across the surface of that lake, the awe-inspiring image of the Tetons would be distorted. In much the same way, the biblical record of Adam's sin reminds us it was at that time when the image of God in man became massively marred.

From that moment forward, man has been involved in a record of non-stop rebellion. First Adam and Eve rebel. Soon Cain rebels, murdering his brother. Later Lot rebels against Abraham. Esau rebels against Jacob. Absalom rebels against King David, his father. Down to this day, nothing has changed. "All have sinned and come short of the glory of God." All are in rebellion against the teachings of God.

The Fall of Man and the Universality of Sin

Therefore, just as sin came into the world through man, and death through sin, so death spread to all men because all sinned. †Romans 5:12

CHILDREN ALWAYS HAVE FOUND NURSERY rhymes to be fun to recite. One of the all-time favorites goes like this:

> Humpty Dumpty sat on a wall,
> Humpty Dumpty had a great fall;
> All the king's horses and all the king's men
> Could not put Humpty Dumpty together again.

The words sound silly, but they actually have an affinity to the message of Romans 5:12-21. The biblical record of Genesis 3 describes a historic event. It centers on a real man by the name of Adam. He was the progenitor of the human race. As a consequence, Adam was appointed by God as the representative of the human race.

If Adam obeyed God, both he and his descendants would enjoy God's gracious benefits. If he disobeyed, it was equally true that he and all his offspring would be involved in a far reaching calamity.

> No one likes the label "sinner" yet it is a title that cannot be avoided.

Going back to our Humpty Dumpty rhyme, Adam, in effect, sat on a kind of "symbolic wall." It was a wall of innocence. It was a wall typifying man's perfect fellowship with God. But, like Humpty Dumpty, Adam also experienced a catastrophic fall. It was a fall from which no one was able to deliver him—no one but the God-appointed Savior.

Unlike the fatal fall of Humpty Dumpty, in the case of Adam, Romans 5 introduces an ominous message. It centers on the *universality of sin*. Sin is not a favorite subject of Adam's race. No one likes the label "sinner." Yet, it is a title that cannot be avoided.

Most would freely admit they are not absolutely good. They also would add, that neither are they all that bad. They would prefer to think of themselves as basically "good people." Do they fall short of their desires to be a better people? Sure! Many would contend that their disagreeable deeds simply mean they have not had sufficient opportunity to develop their better qualities.

Others, if they do get caught in bad behavior, may protest, it is the result of injustices they have had to live with. But whatever the response, seldom is there a willingness to admit the problem exists within us.

Alexander Solzenitsyn did not share in such an optimistic assessment of the human condition. In writing The Gulag Archipelago, he commented: "If only there were evil people somewhere insidiously committing evil deeds, and it were necessary only to separate them from the rest of us and destroy them. But the line dividing good and evil cuts through the heart of every human being. And who is willing to destroy a piece of his own heart?"

The philosopher Pascal was equally lacking in an optimistic view of the human condition. "We are at the same time, creatures of the highest grandeur and the worst misery. We are able to contemplate a better life, one we cannot achieve." So, what is our problem? Jesus answered this way: "...no good tree bears bad fruit." Since the fruit of our lives is not good, says Jesus, we are forced to look for the problem in the tree itself. The cause of the human condition, says Romans 5, is to be found in the fact that *all mankind is ruined by sin.*

Man's dilemma is a bit like trying to drive an automobile with a twisted axle. If the axle is twisted, the wheels always will be out of alignment. As a consequence, the car always will go off course. In effect, every person coming into the world does so with a "twisted axle." Every person has a sin-dominated mind. As a consequence, each of us also move far from the path of God's choosing. We have a bias to disobedience. It goes to the very core of our being.

Sin Permeates the Core of Our Life

The Lord saw that the wickedness of man was great in the earth, and that every intention of the thoughts of his heart was only evil continually. †Genesis 6:5

They have all turned aside; together they have become corrupt; there is none who does good, not even one. †Psalm 14:3

For all have sinned and fall short of the glory of God. †Romans 3:23

Every individual is totally inclined toward sin.

WHEN THE BIBLE SAYS ALL mankind are sinners, it is not just saying they commit sins. Their problem is deeper than that. It is more crippling and profound. The Bible is saying every individual is totally inclined toward sin. Even an unbelieving scientist such as Albert Einstein was compelled to say, "It is easier to denature plutonium than to denature the evil spirit of man." All people want to sin. It is in their spiritual DNA.

Scripture also speaks to the fact that man's deformity is not passive. He rebels against the desires of God because he wants to be in charge. It is an eager yet sinful ambition that penetrates to the core of man's being. "Those who are in the flesh cannot please God" (Romans 8:7, 8). It also, said Jesus, is why, "No one can come to me, unless the Father who sent me draws him" (John 6:44).

People cannot come to Christ because they are totally without power. Ephesians 2 describes man's unresponsive spiritual condition as a form of *death*. When Genesis 6:5 says, "Every intention of the thoughts of man's heart is only evil continually," it is depicting the *extent* of the damage done as a consequence of Adam's rebellion. It is saying every part of the nature of mankind has been contaminated by the fall of Adam. Because of one man's action, a demoralizing defilement has entered into the spiritual bloodstream of all mankind.

"Take a glass of water. Stir in a teaspoon of deadly poison. The whole glass of water is ruined. But it could be ruined even more by adding another teaspoon of poison, and then another, and another. However, one teaspoon does spread the deadly poison throughout." (G.I. Williamson, The Westminster Confession of Faith for Study Classes)

Again, it is because of Adam's disobedience that the Bible now describes mankind as being "dead in trespasses and sins." It also is why, "No one seeks for God ... Together they have become worthless, no one does good, not even one" (Romans 3:10-12). Once more, it is because everyone coming into the world since Adam is "spiritually dead" that Jesus is compelled to say, "No man can come to me unless the Father draws him" (John 6:44).

Ephesians 2 describes man's unresponsive spiritual condition as a form of death.

Tragically, the consequences of Adam's sin have been both universal and devastating. "...Sin came into the world through one man, and death through sin, so death spread to all men because all sinned" (Romans 5:12).

Adam Is the Federal Head of the Human Race

Therefore, as one trespass led to condemnation for all men, so one act of righteousness leads to justification and life for all men. For as by one man's disobedience the many were made sinners, so by the one man's obedience the many will be made righteous. †**Romans 5:18,19**

THE MESSAGE OF ROMANS 5 is clear: Both man's dilemma and man's deliverance are wrapped up in one word, *solidarity*. Man's condemnation stands in solidarity with Adam. In a similar way, man's salvation stands in solidarity with Jesus Christ.

It is this very representative principle of solidarity that runs through all of life. For example, those who were citizens of the United States on December. 7, 1941 may not have been present when Congress took action to declare war on the Axis powers. But their representatives acted for them. Therefore, it was *their* action. They were implicated in all the consequences of the action.

In much the same fashion, along with Adam, all mankind became guilty sinners in the Garden of Eden. All mankind was not physically present in that garden. But mankind's representative was there. Adam acted in their place. As a consequence, they too, were driven out from the garden. They too, were excluded from "the tree of life."

> Both man's dilemma and man's deliverance are wrapped up in one word: solidarity.

It is a principle that can be seen in many dimensions of life. For example, at the time when Albert Einstein published his theory of relativity, few people even understood the implications of what he was proposing. But today, all mankind has been ushered into the atomic age. All mankind is left to live with the consequences of what one man introduced into the world.

Joshua 7 presents yet another graphic illustration of this solidarity principle. Because of the sin of Achan, the whole nation was branded as sinful. The whole nation also was punished by God. Achan could not be separated from the mass of his people. There was solidarity.

> Adam is put before all men as their representative. If he makes it, they make it! If he does not make it, neither do they.

In a similar way, that is the message of Romans 5. Adam is put before all men as their representative. If he makes it, they make it! If he does not make it, neither do they!

In fact, without an understanding of this principle of solidarity, neither can there be an understanding of what man's salvation is all about. It is this same concept of solidarity that not only brings about man's desperate human condition; it also introduces man to God's saving mercy in Christ Jesus.

Jesus. "The second Adam." Reverses the Curse

For as in Adam all die, so all in Christ shall be made alive.
†I Corinthians 15:22

INTO MAN'S PREDICAMENT COMES MAN'S Redeemer. As all mankind stands in solidarity with Adam, so all who are believers stand in solidarity with Jesus Christ. The Savior is described in Scripture as "the second Adam." He comes to man's dilemma in a blaze of glory. Jesus offers to God His perfect obedience. It is a perfect righteousness. It is a perfect goodness. Those for whom the Savior dies are ruined by sin. They also are rescued by the "Spotless Lamb of God."

> As all mankind stands in solidarity with Adam, so all who are believers stand in solidarity with Jesus Christ. The Savior is described in Scripture as "the second Adam".

The rescue is far reaching. When the Savior confronts man's crisis, forgiveness is just the first step.

Because the redeemed become one in Christ Jesus, "old things are passed away, behold, all things are become new" (II Corinthians 5:17). Those in Christ Jesus become members of a new race of people. They become forever God's people. They become eternally secure. There is no "in and out" process involved in their salvation.

"As in Adam all die, so all in Christ shall be made alive" (I Corinthians 15:22). It is the very reason Charles Wesley wrote:

> Thou, O Christ, art all I want,
> More than all in Thee I find.

"One trespass led to condemnation for all men ...By one man's disobedience, the many were made sinners" (Romans 5:18, 19). Those ruined by the fall have been delivered. They have been rescued because of the righteousness of Christ.

Those rescued stand in solidarity with the Savior. He has reversed the curse! "By one man's obedience the many will be made righteous" (Romans 5:18, 19). All their sins are blotted out. God declares them to be acceptable in His holy sight. They are reconciled to God. They are clothed with the righteousness of Christ Jesus.

> *God's saints stand in solidarity with their Savior. All of the evil they have ever done is placed on Jesus. All the perfect purity and righteousness of Jesus is forever placed on them.*

God's grace truly is amazing. Reconciled sons and daughters cannot be silent. They are irresistibly compelled to sing with the psalmist, "...of the steadfast love of the Lord forever" (Psalm 89:1). His pardoning grace is rich and free. Nothing could be of greater importance than this!

The Savior does so much more than save those who are in Him. He does so much more than "keep them in all their ways." He makes them to be "a royal priesthood" (I Peter 2:9). He anoints them to rule with Him forever and ever. It is the very message of Revelation 1:6. Christ Jesus has "...made (them) unto God kings and priests; and (they) shall reign on the earth." With clear voice or with croaking voice, they rejoice to sing:

> Changed from glory into glory
> 'Till in heaven we take our place;
> 'Till we cast our crowns before Thee,
> Lost in wonder, love and praise.

When folks talk about the glory of the gospel, all of this is what they are pointing to. God's saints stand in solidarity with their Savior. All of the evil they have ever done is placed on Jesus. All the perfect purity and righteousness of Jesus is forever placed on them.

Wonder of wonders, the Savior has come to broken lives. Hallelujah! What a Savior! He has put broken lives back together again.

FOOD FOR THOUGHT

"Blessings and battles, daylight and darkness, testimony and trial are all part of the grand providence by which God reveals himself to a world in need. By troubles God keeps us from dependence upon the false comforts of this world. In the darkness He reminds us of how much we need His light... With the blessing He bestows despite our weaknesses, He draws our hearts to Him and paints the grace that redeems a great multitude. His providence will vary with the nature of the soul He has determined to reach, but His purpose is fixed. God will redeem His people. His ways are never meaningless." QUOTES 16

QUESTIONS FOR FEEDBACK

1. Looking at Genesis 3:7-15, what three blessings did Adam lose when he sinned?

2. In Genesis 3, Satan tempted Adam and Eve with the question, "Did God really say?" How might someone today fall prey to that same question?

3. How does the average person react to the message that he or she is born with a sinful nature?

4. From Romans 5:10-15, list what is true of a man "in Christ" and a man "in Adam."

5. How has the sin of Adam affected his descendants to the present day?

6. Is it accurate to describe the believer today as being both "the old man" and "the new man?" Can you confirm your answer from Scripture?

CHAPTER 6

LIFE IS NEVER QUE SERA SERA

"Were there no election, there would be no calling, and
no conversions, and all evangelistic activity would fail. But
as it is, we know as we spread God's truth, that his word will
not return to him void. He has sent it to be the means whereby
he calls his elect, and it will prosper in the thing for which
he has sent it." QUOTES #17

IN EARLIER GENERATIONS PEOPLE READILY recognized God's governance in the affairs of men. Benjamin Franklin wrote, "The longer I live, the more convincing proofs I see of this truth, that God governs in the affairs of men"

Andrew Jackson, elected to the presidency of the United States in 1828, was a powerful persona. A battle hardened warrior, He also was an outspoken believer in the providence of God. When his daughter lay gravely ill, he wrote to her husband: "I trust in the mercy of a kind superintending Providence, that He will restore her to health."

Before issuing the Emancipation Proclamation, Abraham Lincoln wrote, "It is my earnest desire to know the will of Providence in this matter. And if I learn what it is, I will do it."

Before taking his soldiers into harm's way, the brilliant and godly "Stonewall" Jackson, general of the Confederate Army, told his men, "The battle is ours. The outcome belongs to Providence. It is of God."

Those are sentiments we do not often hear today. Instead, when thinking about future happenings, what many will remember is a celebrated song introduced in the mid 20th Century by Doris Day: "Que Sera, Sera, whatever will be will be."

The song was first sung in the Alfred Hitchcock movie, The Man Who Knew Too Much. As a matter of record, the popular tune won an Academy Award for best original song.

The words Doris Day sang expressed the notion that, whatever happens in life, those circumstances are ruled by independent, natural forces. It is a sentiment shared by many, but not by God's Word.

God Ordains Whatever Comes To Pass

Many are the plans in the mind of a man, but it is the purpose of the Lord that will stand. †Proverbs 19:21

> My counsel shall stand, and I will accomplish all my purpose... I have spoken, and I will bring it to pass; I have proposed and I will do it.
> †Isaiah 46:10, 11

THIS GRACIOUS OUTWORKING OF GOD'S purpose is a basic assertion of the Bible. Nothing happens by chance. The message of Genesis 41:32 is quite clear: God upholds, guides, and governs all circumstances. He "works out everything in conformity with the purpose of his will" (Ephesians 1:11). God reigns. He exercises total dominion over great and small. He wills as He chooses. He also carries out all that He wills. The very stability of all creation is guaranteed by this providential rule of God.

> *Nothing happens by chance... God upholds, guides and governs all circumstances*

In the Sermon on the Mount Jesus taught this very truth. Even something as seemingly inconsequential as the flight and fall of a tiny sparrow is within God's providential will and control. According to our Savior, the events of life happen according to God's irresistible decree. "God does according to His will in the host of heaven and among the inhabitants of the earth; and no one can ward off his hand or say to him, what have you done" (Daniel 4:34,35).

For finite, fallen man such providential control can call forth controversy. But for the believer, God's sovereign decrees bring profound relief. It is a source of great gratitude to know that "all things work together for good to those who love God and are called according to his purpose" (Romans 8:28). God's sovereign decrees speak to the fact that in both good times and bad, the life of the Christian is mercifully tied to Jesus,

> *The very stability of all creation is guaranteed by this providential rule of God.*

the one who loves with an everlasting love. He is their Defender. Their Redeemer. Their Friend.

Whatever God Creates God Sustains

The king's heart is a stream of water in the hand of the Lord; He turns it wherever he will. †**Proverbs 21:1**

In him we have obtained an inheritance, having been predestined according to the purpose of him who works all things according to the counsel of His will. †**Ephesians 1:11**

THE WORLD AT LARGE MAY bravely sing, "Que Sera, Sera," but it really isn't so! Meaningless change never will replace God's purposeful order. If it did, pandemonium would reign supreme. Not a very comforting thought!

As created beings, do men and women have a degree of freedom? Absolutely, but it is not an absolute autonomy. They are free within limits established by God's perfect wisdom. Do they, at times, refuse to acknowledge God, and worship God, and be thankful to God? Obviously they do! But when they do, look out! Scripture teaches that a rebellious mindset ends up causing man to be launched on a path leading to grim consequences. Romans 1:22 puts it this way: "Claiming to be wise, they became fools."

> *A rebellious mindset ends up causing man to be launched on a path leading to grim consequences.*

So, for the redeemed of the Lord, what is it that God brings about by "...the free and immutable counsel of His will"? It is this: He brings about His loving purpose for His adopted sons and daughters. When the Christian reads Ephesians 2:4, God is described as being "rich in mercy because of the great love with which he loved us." That is a comforting message.

The tender mercy and the steadfast love of God guarantees that His goodness will follow, all the days of our lives. Such providential care and control brings what John Calvin describes as, "Gratitude of mind for the favorable outcome of things, patience in adversity, and also incredible freedom from worry about the future..." (The Institutes of the Christian Religion).

The Bible's message confirming God's providential decrees is the very antithesis of "Que Sera, Sera." So-called "chance happenings" are an illusion. Chance speaks of impersonal, cold mathematical possibilities. Our God is not impersonal. And He certainly cannot be pictured as a cold deity. The God of the Bible is the fountain of all hope. What He plans, He performs. What He designs, He carries out. He guarantees, "...a future and a hope" for those who walk in His ways.

God's Loving Heart Embraces "Concurrence"

As for you, you meant evil against me; but God meant it for good...
† Genesis 50:19

This Jesus, delivered up according to the definite plan and foreknowledge of God, you crucified and killed by the hands of lawless men.
† Acts 2:23

CONCURRENCE DESCRIBES EVENTS THAT HAPPEN together. Events that converge. Events that happen side by side. In terms of God's all wise and loving providence, concurrence points to the coming together of the actions of God, alongside the actions of man.

We are people with a will of our own. Both for good and for bad, we are a people who cause things to happen. But what also is true is this: the power we exercise is a secondary power. It remains under God's providential control. From a biblically informed perspective, concurrence says that God works out

His perfect will through the imperfect, if not evil, actions of human wills.

For example, in Genesis 45-50, the brothers of Joseph were guilty of treacherous deeds. Yet, God's providence continued to be at work. As a consequence, in Genesis 50:20, Joseph tells his brothers,"...as for you, you meant evil against me; but God meant it for good in order to bring it about, as it is this day, to save many people alive." That's concurrence in action!

In terms of God's all wise and loving providence, concurrence points to the coming together of the actions of God, alongside the actions of man.

The story of Ruth, the Moabite, is another example of concurrence. It was forbidden in Scripture for a Jew to marry a Moabite. It was a sin! When Ruth married Naomi's son, a transgression was committed against the revealed will of God. At the same time, God's providential purposes were still being carried out. Marriage exposed Ruth to the God of the Bible. Eventually, she made the decision to serve the one true God. As a consequence, this favored woman speaks unforgettable words of faith and commitment, "Your people shall be my people and your God my God" (Ruth 1:16). Once more, Ruth's experience reflects concurrence in action.

David is yet another example of the action of men and the actions of God coming together. Throughout his life, Israel's king suffered greatly because of the sins of others. Yet, in spite of their treacherous deeds, David sees the hand of his God. In fact, what he observed moved him to write some magnificent psalms, testifying to His ever deepening faith in God. For example, Psalm 3 reflects David's response when he fled from Absalom. "Lord, how they have increased who trouble me! Many are they who rise up against me. Many are they who say of me,

'There is no help for him in God,' but you, O Lord, are a shield for me, my glory and the one who lifts up by head."

By far, the greatest example of concurrence centers on the sin of many against the spotless Lamb of God. They hated our Savior for His holiness. They wanted to eliminate the *Lord of glory*. They also failed! They failed because once more, God turned this greatest of all evils to the greatest of all blessings.

> God works through the sinful actions of men to bring forth unimaginable good.

In all such examples demonstrating concurrence in action, God works through the sinful actions of men to bring forth unimaginable good. God performs His deeds of deliverance in keeping with His eternal providential purposes. The reality of concurrence repeatedly assures the believer that even when the sins of others bring unhappiness, God never stops working. The Heavenly Father never stops working in ways that cannot always be seen. Concurrence continues to be in play.

Because it is, the Christian can be certain that his faulty vision does not change reality. God is working to bring about His perfect purposes in the lives of His people.

God's Providence Inescapably Also Points to His sovereignty

The Lord of hosts has sworn, as I have planned, so shall it be, and as I have proposed, so shall it stand. †Isaiah 14:24

ON ONE OCCASION, THE APOSTLE Peter announced that Jesus was "...delivered up by the determined counsel and foreknowledge of God." In making that statement, he was emphasizing this: God is the one who ultimately controls even the details of His

Son's destiny. All that happens, be it good or bad, is within the perfect will of God or the permissive will of God.

Coming back to the Sermon on the Mount, Jesus made it clear: God knows all about contingencies in life. He even knows about such things as birds falling from the sky and hairs falling from our head. As a matter of fact, God does not just wait patiently for these contingencies to take place. Before they happen, our God knows how He will respond. Jesus taught that God's loving control over the believer's life is complete. It is a reality that has everything to do with God's sovereign and compassionate providence.

> *Jesus taught that God's loving control over the believer's life is complete. It is a reality that has everything to do with God's sovereign and compassionate providence.*

The Language of Grace Dominates The Providential Actions of God

God... saved us and called us to a holy calling not because of our works but because of his own purpose and grace. † **II Timothy 1:9**

When the goodness and lovingkindness of God our Savior appeared, he saved us, not because of works done by us in righteousness, but according to his own mercy, by the Holy Spirit ...so that being justified by his grace, we might become heirs according to the hope of eternal life. † **Titus 2:4-7**

THE LANGUAGE OF GOD'S PROVIDENCE is the language of God's grace. It has nothing in common with the fatalistic grip of blind fate. It is light years removed from "Que Sera, Sera." Most especially when we contemplate God's marvelous saving grace, never are we to imagine that salvation is left to the faulty wisdom and will of man! To think such a thing is to say, "Whatever will be, will be." That cannot be! From beginning to end, saving grace centers on the definitive actions of God. "Those whom He predestined He also called, and those whom He called He also justified" (Romans 8:30).

At the same time, God never sets aside man's responsibility. He never violates the message of Romans 10:9 and 10: "If you confess with your mouth that Jesus Christ is Lord and believe in your heart that God raised Him from the dead, you will be saved... For everyone who calls on the name of the Lord will be saved."

> Man's actions and man's will become the very "arenas" in which God's initiating power is worked out.

Yet, it is only because God acts that man also must act. That again, is concurrence! Outwardly, man seems to be doing the initiating—but not really! Scripture says it is God who predestines. It is God who effectually calls. It is God who regenerates. It is God who justifies. And it is because of God's saving actions that man also is moved to take action.

Man's actions and man's will become the very "arenas" in which God's initiating power is worked out. "It is God who works in us, both to will and to do of His good pleasure" (Philippians 2:13). It is with just such a sense of concurrent reality in mind that the hymn writer was moved to pen these words:

> I sought the Lord, and afterward I knew
>   He moved my soul to seek Him, seeking me.
> It was not I that found, O Savior true,
>   No, I was found of Thee.
> Thou dids't reach forth Thy hand and mine enfold;
>   I walked and sank not on the storm vexed sea,
> 'Twas not so much that I on Thee took hold,
>   As Thou, dear Lord, on me.
>
> —George Chadwick

The words of that hymn are simply confirming what Scripture teaches. It is not man's faith, or man's repentance, or man's calling on the name of the Lord that becomes the chargeable cause of salvation. Sometimes Christians will say, "The only thing we contribute to our salvation is our faith." It is an understandable sentiment. But it also is not a fully accurate statement. Granted! The Bible repeatedly demands the necessity of faith in the finished work of Christ. It is an undeniable necessity. "To the one who does not work, but trusts him who justifies the ungodly *His faith* is counted as righteousness" (Romans 4:5).

> *Necessary as it is, faith contributes nothing, in the sense of merit to a person's acceptance before a holy God. Rather, faith reaches out and receives what God gives.*

"We know that a person is not justified by works of the law but through *faith* in Jesus Christ" (Galatians 2:16). And in Ephesians 2:8, "For by grace you have been saved through *faith*..." Faith is necessary because it is through faith that man rests upon the finished work of Christ.

But necessary as it is, faith contributes nothing, in the sense of merit to a person's acceptance before a holy God. Rather, faith reaches out and receives what God gives. Faith receives the forgiveness that comes through the atoning work of Christ. Faith trusts in the saving promise of God. As a matter of fact, the faith required by God also is a faith given by God. It is part of the Holy Spirit's work of regeneration.

> *The faith required by God also is a faith given by God. It is part of the Holy Spirit's work of regeneration.*

Are people justified by faith alone? Most certainly they are! But at the same time, this faith given by God is only a saving faith because it is utterly dependent on the finished work of Christ. Faith does not save. Only Jesus saves!

If one is saved, it is God alone who does the saving. Furthermore, God does the saving as a consequence of His sovereign providential decree. Admittedly that is not a happy thought for some of God's people. They resist what the Bible repeatedly emphasizes: namely, God's predestinating power that moves upon the heart of those who are "spiritually dead" and enables them to reach out and receive the gift of God's saving mercy in Christ Jesus. It is only this action on the part of God that gives the peace and confidence to know: "He who began a good work in us will also perfect that work 'till the day of Christ" (Philippians 1:6).

Ever since Adam rebelled and fell from God's grace, the heart of man has been hardened by willful sin. Man now can act only according to his fallen nature. He has no desire to truly repent. He has no desire to cast himself upon God's saving mercy. It is the very reason why Jesus said, "No one can come to me unless the Father who sent me draws him" (John 6:44). Without an enabling that comes only from God, salvation is never going to happen.

Dr. Harry Ironside, one of the great Bible teachers of the 20th Century, once told a true story about a man who testified to how God sought him, and found him, and saved him. It was a moving testimony to the glory of God. After the meeting, however, someone took the man aside and said, "I appreciated all you said about what God did for you, but you didn't tell us about what you did. You should have mentioned something about your part." "Oh," the man said, "I apologize. I really should have mentioned that my part was running away. God's part was running after me, until He found me."

It's a true testimony. It also illustrates a fundamental, saving truth. It is the language of God's grace that always will dominate

God's providential decree relating to man's salvation. In fact, it is this providential, sovereign grace of God that compels the apostle Paul to write: "Oh, the depth of the riches and wisdom and knowledge of God! How unsearchable are His judgments and how inscrutable His ways! For from Him, and through Him, and to Him are all things. To Him be glory forever. Amen" (Romans 11:33, 36).

Christian: the language of God's amazing grace never can be diminished. Always God's sovereign saving action will dominate in the affairs of man. Life is never *Que Sera, Sera*!

FOOD FOR THOUGHT

"The Bible never tries to hide evil from us. God offers no sugar-coating on suffering—no mystical sleight of hand—to pretend this reality is not as it seems… The Bible says frustration and suffering exist in our world because Adam disobeyed God… Human sin led to earth's misery. The perfect world God created was corrupted by the evil for which Adam and Eve were responsible… The God of the Bible is neither silent, savage, nor still with regard to evil. In His Word He says a perfect world was corrupted by man. In His providence He uses the consequences of sin in this world to draw His children into His embrace. In His mercy He sent His Son to save mankind from the sinful suffering of which man himself is the cause." QUOTES #18

QUESTIONS FOR FEEDBACK

1. Why is there no chance that an unconverted individual will do the will of God or that a converted individual will not begin to do the will of God?

2. Can you cite three passages of Scripture that present a strong case for believing that God controls everything?

3. Why should the Christian thank God every day that salvation is because of God's sovereign grace alone?

4. What do you think of the following statement: "Election is the strongest possible encouragement to evangelize"?

5. In what way does a believer experience comfort and joy in knowing that God is sovereign?

6. Can you list some of the objections often given for not believing in God's absolute sovereignty? Can you answer why these objections are not scriptural?

LIFE IS NEVER QUE SERA SERA

CHAPTER 7

GOD'S FINGER ON MAN'S SHOULDER

"It is this Abrahamic Covenant, so explicitly set forth in Genesis 15 and 17 that underlies the whole subsequent development of God's redemptive promise, word and action. It is in terms of the promise given to Abraham, that in him and his seed all the families of the earth would be blessed, that God sent forth His Son in the fullness of time in order that He might redeem them that were under the law and all without distinction might receive the adoption of sons. It is in fulfillment of this promise to Abraham that there is now no longer Jew or Gentile, male nor female, bond nor free… and that all believers are blessed with faithful Abraham." QUOTES #19

THE ACADEMY AWARD FILM THE Soloist is one of those movies not easily dismissed from one's thoughts. It tells a tale that is riveting. A Los Angeles Newspaper columnist descends to the homeless streets of L. A., where he discovers a brilliant musician. This man is hopelessly lost in the dark, destructive world of mental illness. He cannot escape from his desperate dungeon of despair.

To say that the journalist is impacted would be an understatement. In spite of repeated rejection, the reporter relentlessly pursues his new found friend. He cannot and will not forsake him. The love demonstrated for this hapless musician is overwhelming. It is Active. Invincible. Unchanging.

The friendship epitomizes an implacable compassion and a resolute mercy. It is relentless. Unyielding. Undiminished. In fact, this bond of friendship transforms the lives of both men.

Implications of Covenant Grace

We bring the good news that what God promised to the fathers, this He has fulfilled to us their children by raising Jesus. †Acts 13:32-33

Is God the God of Jews only? Is he not the God of Gentiles also? Yes, Gentiles also, since God is one. He will justify the circumcised by faith and the uncircumcised through faith. †Romans 3:29-30

If you are Christ's then are you Abraham's offspring, heirs according to promise. †Galatians 3:29

THE BIBLE PICTURES GOD'S RELATIONSHIP with His covenant people as built upon just such a presupposition of unimaginable friendship and unforgettable mercy. God comes into their darkness. He comes to "seek and to save those who are lost." He comes to give what His people most need. They will become "vessels of God's mercy" (Romans 9:23). It will be a mercy given abundantly. It will overflow. It will have no end.

When difficulties increase, God will sustain His covenant people. When weariness distorts their perspective, He will strengthen them. When friends are unfaithful, God will be their "Friend in need."

"No longer do I call you servants," says Jesus. "I have called you *friends*" (John 15:15). He is that friend who "sticks closer than a brother" (Proverbs 18:24). He is that friend "who loves at *all times*" (Proverbs 17:17). He "lays down his life for his friends" (John 15:12).

> Who of all our friends to save us
> > Could or would have shed his blood?
> But the Savior died to have us
> > Reconciled to Him in God.
> This was boundless love indeed;
> > Jesus is a *friend in need*.
>
> **—John Newton**

And to what point does Scripture trace this friendship and mercy of God? It is traced all the way back to its source in God's everlasting covenant of grace. With unbreakable cords, God has bound Himself by covenant oath to those who are "Abraham's seed and heirs according to the promise." And who are they? Galatians 3:29 answers that question: "If you are Christ's then you are Abraham's offspring, heirs according to promise."

God has descended into the darkness of the spiritual dungeon in which we were imprisoned. He has come with His message of covenantal compassion: "I will be your God and you will be my people." It is a solemn vow. An everlasting

Without an appreciation of God's covenantal friendship, never can we fully appreciate the amazing grace of God's redeeming love.

vow. An unbreakable vow. It is boundless love indeed; Jesus is a friend in need.

In fact, without an appreciation of God's covenantal friendship, never can we fully appreciate the amazing grace of God's redeeming love. It is God's finger on our shoulder. Lost and undeserving as we are, God extends the greatest of dignities to covenantal sons and daughters. They are adopted into His royal household.

Once they were homeless "castaways." They were "foreigners to the covenant of promise" (Ephesians 2:11). Now, they are hid with God in Christ. They have all the rights and privileges of God's forever family. They are "fellow citizens with the saints and members of the household of God" (Ephesians 2:12-13).

> *Never do God's covenantal people need to be anxious or afraid.*

Former homeless "castaways" are now connected! They are blessed with the most intimate of relationships with Jesus, "the friend of sinners." But that's not all! As His covenant children, they also now enjoy the experience of a refreshing relationship with newly discovered brothers and sisters in Christ. They now are part of God's loving covenantal family. In fact, their connectedness extends even further.

By historic succession, they now experience the transforming sense of dignity and destiny that is the result of knowing they are united with God's covenantal people throughout the ages. They are connected by covenantal commitment to Abraham, Moses, David, Miriam, Ruth, and Naomi. They are connected to Paul, Barnabas, Peter and John. They are connected to Mary, Martha, Dorcas and Phoebe.

God's covenantal children are connected by covenantal promises. Never will they be abandoned by their covenant keeping God. "He spreads his wings over them even as an eagle overspreads her young. She carries them upon her wings as does the Lord his people" (Deuteronomy 32:11).

Never do God's covenantal people need to be anxious or afraid. God's grace will be their portion. "I am your God," says El Shaddai. "I will strengthen you; I will help you. I will uphold you with my victorious right hand" (Isaiah 41:10).

God's covenantal people always will be refreshed by His patient, forgiving love. It is why Micah the prophet asks, "Where is another God like you who pardons the sins of his people?" And then he gives us this word of assurance: "You will tread our sins beneath your feet; you will throw them into the depths of the ocean... You will set your love upon us, as you promised our father Abraham" (Micah 7:18).

> *God encourages His people to respond to others in the same way He has responded to them.*

Such is the very nature of our covenant keeping God. His sensitive heart always moves out to His redeemed people. He causes them to experience all that it means to be a new people in Christ Jesus. A major part of what that means is this: God encourages His people to respond to others in the same way He has responded to them.

» Enthusiastically, they are to demonstrate unconditional love to others.
» Empathetically, they are to extend forgiveness to others.
» Eagerly, they are to listen to the cries of others.
» Earnestly, they are to be patient with others. In all such actions they lift up the language of covenantal kindness.

God's saving Grace Is Covenantal Grace

And Mary said, 'my soul magnifies the Lord, and my spirit rejoices in God my Savior... He has helped his servant Israel, in remembrance of his mercy, as he spoke to our fathers, to Abraham and to his offspring forever.' †Luke 1:46-47; 54-55

> We say that faith was counted to Abraham as righteousness... He received the sign of circumcision as a seal of the righteousness that he had by faith while he was still uncircumcised... The purpose was to make him the father of all who believe without being circumcised, so that righteousness would be counted to them as well. †**Romans 4:9-11**

AN UNDERSTANDING OF GOD'S COVENANT promise to Abraham will help God's called out people today to appreciate more fully the transforming wonder of God's redeeming grace in Christ Jesus. It is the very reason God's people sing:

> A debtor to mercy alone
> > Of covenant mercy I sing;
> Nor fear, with Thy righteousness on,
> > My person and offering to bring.
>
> —**Augustus Toplady**

It is God's ancient covenantal commitment that moved the heart of the apostle Paul to instruct believers in Galatians, that "the Scripture foreseeing that God would justify the Gentiles by faith, preached the gospel beforehand to Abraham." He was reminding Gentiles in Galatia that they worship and serve the God of Abraham, Isaac, and Jacob, who has pledged Himself to their full redemption. This is the reason God vowed: "Behold, my covenant is with you (Abraham), and you shall be the father of a multitude of nations."

From Genesis to Revelation, God's Salvation Is a Covenantal Salvation

He remembers his covenant forever... the covenant he had with Abraham as an everlasting covenant. †**I Chronicles 16:15-17**

Jerusalem will become... a sheepfold offering salvation to a world under judgment. †**Micah 7:20**

> Jew and Gentile... will take their place at the feast with Abraham, Isaac and Jacob, in the kingdom of heaven. †Matthew 8:11

> Your father Abraham rejoiced to see my day. He saw it and was glad. †John 8:56

WHEN GOD ANNOUNCED TO ABRAHAM, "I will be your God and you shall be my people," that covenantal vow became a central, unifying theme throughout Scripture. The following twenty seven examples underscore this very fact.

Genesis 17:4, 7, 8

"Behold, my covenant is with you (Abraham), and you shall be the father of a multitude of nations... and I will establish my covenant between me and you and your offspring after you, throughout their generations for an everlasting covenant, to be God to you and to your offspring after you."

A multitude of Gentile believers from every tribe, language, and nation share in the faith of Abraham. They also participate in this covenant promise (Ephesians 2:11-13). They are spiritually incorporated into Israel.

The covenant promise of Genesis 17 is an everlasting covenant. It endures forever. It endures because God does not change. It endures because Jesus, the Messenger and Mediator of the covenant, will fulfill every condition of the covenant.

> *Jesus, the Messenger and Mediator of the covenant, will fulfill every condition of the covenant.*

When He comes, He gives substance to the covenant promise. He offers Himself as the final and perfect sacrifice for the sins of a covenant people.

These words of Genesis 17, "...I will be your God and you shall be my people" encapsulate the essence of our salvation to this very day. Without the assurance they communicate, all other promised blessings in the believer's life become empty and worthless.

Exodus 2:24
God's chosen people were delivered from bondage in Egypt in order that they might carry out God's everlasting covenant of saving grace. "God heard their groanings and remembered his covenant with Abraham, with Isaac and with Jacob." God always will be faithful to His covenant promise.

Leviticus 26:42
Punishment for sins committed does not bring an end to God's covenant relationship with individuals. Rather, God amplifies how He will continue to accomplish His covenantal promise. It will happen for God's Old Testament covenant people, through confession of sin and through the Levitical sacrifices ordained by God: "If they confess their iniquities... then I will remember my covenant with Isaac, and my covenant with Abraham."

Deuteronomy 29:12-15
Speaking of the mercy and goodness of God to his chosen people, Moses writes that these character traits of God are grounded in His covenantal promise. "The Lord your God is a merciful God. He will not... forget the covenant with your fathers that he swore to them."

Joshua 7:11
The sin of Achan is extremely serious. It is critical, says God, because Achan has "transgressed my covenant." God is committed to His covenant promise to Abraham. It is of grave importance. As a consequence, the actions of Achan are potentially catastrophic because they threaten the fulfillment of God's covenantal promise.

Judges 2:1,20

God identifies Himself as the covenantal benefactor of His people. As such, He keeps His promise. But the people do not, and as a consequence, they are punished. "The anger of the Lord was kindled against Israel... because this people have transgressed my covenant..."

I Kings 8:23,43

At the dedication of the temple in Jerusalem, Solomon is deeply conscious of the fact that this magnificent structure directly relates to God's covenant promise to Abraham. As such, it is to be a temple that embraces all nations, in fulfillment of God's covenantal promise.

II Kings 13:23

Once more, we are reminded that the Lord is gracious and has compassion "...because of his covenant with Abraham, Isaac, and Jacob." As a consequence of this covenant promise, the commitment of God to His people is steadfast and eternal.

I Chronicles 16:15-17

In David's song of thanksgiving, he sings of how God never will forget what he has vowed to Abraham. God remembers His covenant forever, "...the word he commanded for a thousand generations, the covenant that he made with Abraham."

Nehemiah 9:7,8

The people praise God for choosing Abraham and giving to the patriarch the covenant of promise. "You have kept your promise for you are righteous." They glorify God because it is this covenant which continues to be the basis upon which God always will extend His grace to His redeemed people.

Psalm 105:8-10

Once more, communicating through the psalmist, God reaffirms His covenantal relationship with the spiritual descendants of Abraham. "He remembers his covenant forever, the word that he commanded for a thousand generations, the covenant that He swore with Abraham."

Isaiah 42:1-7

God brings us into His eternal and majestic chamber. Through the prophet Isaiah he writes, "Behold my servant, whom I uphold, my chosen, in whom my soul delights... He will bring forth justice to the nations... a bruised reed he will not break... He will faithfully bring forth justice... I am the Lord; I have called you in righteousness... I will give you *as a covenant* for the people, a light for the nations, to open the eyes of the blind, to bring out... from the prison those who sit in darkness."

> *The Messiah is God's servant who is given "as a covenant" to God's chosen ones... He is the essence of the covenant.*

The prophet is presenting Jesus, the coming Messiah as the very embodiment of all that God's covenant signifies. Messiah is God's servant who is given "as a covenant" to God's chosen ones. As the one who embodies the covenant, he pleases God.

Why? He pleases God because He is the essence of the covenant. The fullness of the covenant. He is the object of Jehovah's love and favor. His universal kingdom is one of justice and righteousness. Isaiah writes, that when this One who is given "as a Covenant," enters the world, He does not break the weak. Instead, He heals the weak. He also comes as "a light for the nations." He is given "as a covenant" because He designs the covenant. He frames the covenant. He takes the promise given to Abraham into His own hand and works out every condition.

Jeremiah 31:31,32

Because of what might be described as limitations of the covenant under the Old Testament dispensation, a vastly improved expression of the covenant is coming in the New Testament dispensation. No longer will there be types and shadows representing significant elements of the covenantal gospel message. This promised new covenant is to be a perfection of the old. And yet, the benediction of Hebrews speaks of the fact that it remains God's "everlasting covenant." For this very reason, the declaration of Genesis 17 is repeated in Jeremiah 3:33. It is a particular declaration serving as the summary of God's promised everlasting blessings: "I will be their God, and they shall be my people."

Micah 5:2. 4; 7:20

Micah prophesies that God will raise up a ruler from David's descendants who will reign forever. He will fulfill God's covenantal vow to Abraham. "But you, O Bethlehem Ephratah… from you shall come forth for me one who is to be ruler in Israel, whose origin is from of old, from ancient days… He shall stand, and shepherd his flock in the strength of the Lord… He shall be great to the ends of the earth… You will show faithfulness to Jacob and steadfast love to Abraham, as you have sworn to our fathers from the days of old."

Malachi 3:1; 4:2, 5, 6

Malachi prophesies that because of God's covenant oath to Jacob and to Abraham, Jerusalem will become "a sheepfold offering salvation to a world under judgment."

Malachi goes on to say, "The Lord whom you seek, shall suddenly come to his temple, even the messenger of the covenant, whom you delight in" (Malachi 3:1). Scripture repeatedly affirms, it is because of the coming of this Messenger of the covenant, that God is reconciled. Peace is established. Grace is purchased. Heaven's gates are opened wide.

"The sun of righteousness shall rise with healing in His wings. You shall go out leaping like calves from the stall. Behold, I will send you Elijah the prophet before the great and awesome day of the Lord comes. And he will turn the hearts of the fathers to their children and the hearts of the children to their fathers..." In the gospels of Matthew, Mark and Luke this "Elijah" is none other than John the Baptist. Luke 1:17 therefore repeats the message of Malachi. Malachi prophesies that repentance and turning to God will be seen in the restoration of family relationships. It is something John the Baptist, Malachi's "Elijah," goes forth preaching. It is part of his message: "...prepare the way of the Lord."

> *It is because of the coming of this Messenger of the covenant, that God is reconciled. Peace is established. Grace is purchased. Heaven's gates are opened wide.*

Matthew 1:1; 8:11

In the first verse of the first chapter of the first book in the New Testament, Jesus is presented as this promised Messenger and Mediator of God's covenantal people. He not only is "...the son of David," He also is "...the seed of Abraham." It is because of God's covennat promise, that later, in chapter 8, when King Jesus initiates His future state of glory, Matthew writes that it will be a time when both Jews and Gentiles "...take their place at the feast with Abraham, Isaac and Jacob in the kingdom of heaven."

Mark 1:2

Mark quotes from Isaiah, pointing to John the Baptist as part of God's pre-planned redemptive history, part of God's covenantal dealings with His people. "Behold, I send my messenger before your face, who will prepare your way... prepare the way of the Lord..."

Luke 1:54, 55, 68-75

Mary sings of how "...God has helped his servant Israel, remembering to be merciful to Abraham and his descendants forever, even as he said to our fathers."—Zechariah later echoes Mary's praise: "The God of Israel has come... to remember his holy covenant, the oath he swore to our father Abraham."

John 8:56

In a striking statement, Jesus puts the spotlight on His relationship to God's covenant promise to Abraham. He points to the fact that the spiritual father of all who believe was saved only because he believed God's promise of One who was to come, One who would be God's sacrificial lamb to take away our sins. The apostle Paul testifies, that Abraham had the gospel preached to him, as a consequence of this, Jesus announced, "Your father Abraham rejoiced that he would see my day. He saw it and was glad."

Acts 3:25, 26

When Peter delivers his message at Pentecost, what is it that he tells the citizens of Jerusalem? "You are the sons of the covenant made with your father, saying to Abraham, 'and in your offspring shall *all families* of the earth be blessed'." Peter then reminds the thousands who had gathered, that "...the covenant promise is to you and to your children." Later in Acts, both Steven and Paul emphasise the fact, that those who make up Abraham's spiritual posterity are the ones who place their saving faith in this Jesus who has been raised from the dead.

Romans 4:13-17; 5:8, 9

To Christians in Rome, Paul says this: the covenantal promise of salvation, first revealed to Abraham, is a promise that can only be realized by faith alone. He then writes, that those who "...share the faith of Abraham who is the father of us all," are covenantal people of God. Whether Jew or Gentile, all are Abraham's offspring by faith. "...Christ became a servant to the circumcised to show God's truthfulness, in order to confirm the promise given to the patriarchs and in order that the Gentiles might glorify God for his mercy."

Galatians 3:7, 28, 29

Once more, those who are heirs to God's covenant promise are those who share in Abraham's faith, regardless of whether they are the physical descendants of Abraham. To Christians in Galatia, Paul writes, that God's promise of covenantal blessing also comes upon Gentile believers. "Know then that it is those of faith who are the sons of Abraham... There is neither Jew nor Greek... for you are all one in Christ Jesus. And if you are Christ's then you are Abraham's offspring, heirs according to promise."

Ephesians 2:12-14, 19, 20

Even though God's covenantal promise to Abraham included a vow to bless the nations, for the most part, Gentiles were not aware of this hope, says the apostle. Gentiles well knew, that in the courts of the Jewish temple there was a wall that separated Gentiles from Jews. Gentiles could not enter the inner courts of the temple, that place where the priests performed the sacrifices for sins. And so Paul reminds Gentiles to "...remember that you were at that time... alienated from the commonwealth of Israel and strangers to the covenants of promise." But in the coming of Jesus, the mediator of God's covenant promise to Abraham, "You are no longer strangers and aliens, but you are fellow citizens with the saints." Gentile believers now are "...built upon the foundation of the apostles and prophets." Paul's concern now is that his Gentile readers will grasp the glory of their new-found covenantal position. They are participants, Jew and Gentile together, in the love and the power that their covenantal Redeemer brings to them. No longer are Gentiles "...stangers to the covenants of promise." They have been, "...brought near by the blood of Christ."

Philippians 3:3
Gentile believers have been grafted in to the true Israel of God. They are the heirs of God's covenantal promise to Abraham. And because of this, they may not be physically circumcised like Jews, but they most certainly have received a spiritual circumcision. They are, the true Israel of God. They are, says the apostle, "...the real circumcision who worship by the Spirit of God and glory in Christ Jesus and put no confidence in the flesh."

Hebrews 8:6-11; 9:15; 13:20, 21
As the Mediator of God's covenant promise to Abraham, Jesus brings to believers in this New Testament dispensation, even greater blessings than those experienced in the Old Testament dispensation. It is a covenantal theme that is underscored no less than seventeen times by the writer of Hebrews. He is saying, this: both those under the old covenant message and those under the new covenant promises participate in a grace that may be different in substance, yet it is one and the same covenant under the two dispensations. As a consequence he writes, it is "...the blood of the *everlasting* covenant that makes them perfect, working in them what is well pleasing" to this very God of covenantal promise.

I Peter 1:10-12

Peter's message is one that says, the total implications of this unity of Old and New Testament covenantal people was something that even the prophets did not fully comprehend. Yet, when writing of God's covenantal blessings to Abraham, they nevertheless were aware of this: they "...were serving not themselves but you (Gentiles), in the things that have now been announced to you through those who preached the Holy Spirit..."

Revelation 7:9; 21:3

The goal of God's ancient covenant promise is pictured as the gathering and perfecting of a covenant people. They are a people who come "from every nation, from all tribes, and people and languages."

The unity and continuity of this redemptive, covenantal salvation is further revealed by the apostle John in this descriptive vision. "Behold, the tabernacle of God is with men and he will be with them." God will be with them for one reason: it is because of God's covenantal oath sworn to them by God, through Abraham. In Genesis, the opening book of the Bible, God promises, "I will be their God and they shall be my people." And in Revelation, the closing book of the Bible, it is instructive, that once more, we hear that refrain repeated: "They shall be my people, and God himself shall be with them as their God." In other words, the covenant promises made to those who are "overcomers," in Genesis, are the same promises that now are fulfilled to those who are "overcomers" in the last book of the Bible.

> The covenant promises made to those who are "overcomers" in Genesis, are the very same promises that now are fulfilled to those who are "overcomers" in the last book of the Bible.

In summary, it is this very unifying message of God's covenantal commitment to Abraham that repeatedly comes before us from Genesis through Revelation. It provides nothing less than the central framework for our great salvation. Without God's covenant vow to Abraham, there would be no Savior of sinners and no redemptive promises. It is because of the centrality of this covenant that believers in this New Testament dispensation truly become a set apart people who share in the redemtive destiny of God's Old Testament saints.

Stipulating the Terms of God's Covenantal Saving Grace

For by grace you have been saved through faith. And this is not your own doing; it is the gift of God, not the result of works, so that no one may boast. For we are his workmanship, created in Christ Jesus for good works, which God prepared beforehand, that we should walk in them. †**Ephesians 2:8-10**

God's Covenant Is Unilateral

The covenantal promise highlighted in Genesis 15 and 17 is not an agreement between equals. It is a unilateral arrangement that is not negotiated. In the words of Ephesians 2, it is "not of works lest any man should boast."

In Genesis 15, the "word of the Lord came to Abram in a vision: '*Fear not*, Abram, I am your shield; your reward shall be very great.' But Abram said, 'O Lord God, what will you give me, for I continue childless, and the heir of my house is Eleazer of Damascus?' And Abram said, 'Behold, you have given me no offspring...' And behold, the word of the Lord came to him, 'This man shall not be your heir; your very own son shall be your heir.'"

Because Abram is childless, he questions the sovereign Lord about the overwhelmingly vast inheritance that has been promised him. And in the very first verse of Genesis 15, the message of the Lord comes to Abram in one single word: *Trust*!

Why does God say this? It is because the all-too-human impatience of Abram implies a lack of confidence in God. And that's something true of a lot of us. We often suffer from an underlying anxiety that doesn't seem to go away, no matter how long we have walked with God. The Puritan, Thomas Carlyle, confesses: "I have a natural talent for being in a hurry, which is a very bad talent." Carlyle's problem is not uncommon. As the spiritual children of Abraham, we share in this underlying bent toward anxiety and a lack of trust; we have little patience.

In Genesis 15 Abram has taken things into his own hand. "The heir of my house is Eleazer of Damascus". Later on Abram and Sarai again tragically took their destiny into their own hands. Why? They simply did not believe God was able to keep His promises. Once more, it must be said, that we really are no different. It is because of this natural tendency we all have that we need to take to heart the message of Genesis 15, "The word of the Lord came to Abram... *Fear not*... I am your shield; your reward shall be great."

I once read the following account that relates to this very issue of our all-too-frequent impatience. The author is unknown. It went like this:

> As children bring their broken toys with tears for us to mend, I brought my broken dreams to God because He was my friend. But then, instead of leaving Him in peace to work alone, I hung around and tried to help in ways that were my own. At last, I snatched them back and cried, "How can you be so slow?"
> "My child," He said, "You never let them go."

That's precisely what we all do! We are "programmed" to want to control. We want to witness a speedy resolution to our longings, to take things into our own hands. We want to "re-negotiate." To get involved. However, God's covenants are not negotiated. They are unilateral. They demand trust. "Fear not, Abram, I am your shield: your reward shall be very great."

When we say that God's oath of saving grace is *unilateral*, it is precisely what we see in Genesis 15. In the time of Abram, covenantal oaths were not uncommon. They were confirmed by a ceremony in which animals were cut into two parts along the backbone and placed in two rows. The parties to the oath then would walk *together* into that space between the parts. As they walked, they then would speak the words of the covenant vow they were making to each other. It was an oath that became sacred because of shed blood. The parties were saying, "May what has happened to these slain animals happen to me, if I fail to keep this vow."

However in Genesis 15, there is a critical feature that never occurs in other covenantal vows made in that day. God *alone* passed between the pieces of slain animals (Genesis 15:17). In other words, God was confirming His covenantal vow to Abram *by Himself*. Hebrews 6:13-15 makes particular reference to this: "When God made his promise to Abraham, since there was no one greater for him to swear by, he swore by himself, saying 'I will surely bless you and give you many descendants.' So, after waiting patiently, Abraham received what was promised."

There are also other spiritual realities pictured in that dramatic ceremony of Genesis 15. The smoking firepot that passed between the pieces of slain animals pictured another practice of ancient times. The firepot was symbolic of a small furnace used to purify metals. In I Peter 1:7, the apostle has this in mind when he writes about the trial of our faith being "...of greater worth than gold, which perishes even though refined by fire." And in Genesis 15, God is saying, He will refine His covenant people until He can see Himself in them.

The added torch mentioned in Genesis 15:17 also is instructive. It speaks of God's presence that will give light to His people, so that they will not walk in darkness (John 1:5).

God's Covenant Is Eternal

What God speaks, He performs. He does not change His mind. In the movie *Mary Poppins* the two children, Jane and Michael, are jumping into bed after an incredibly exciting day with the amazing Mary Poppins. This is when Jane asks a question: "Mary Poppins, you won't leave us, will you?" Michael then chimes in, "Will you stay if we promise to be good?" Tucking them in Mary Poppins replies, "Look! That's a piecrust promise. Easily made, and easily broken."

God's covenant promise most assuredly is no "piecrust promise." It is eternal. It will not come to an end. What God says, God does! We see a vivid picture of this in Genesis 17. We read about the ceremony of circumcision, the outward Old Testament sign of God's covenantal relationship with His people. If there is one thing that stands out about circumcision, it has to be the fact that it is permanent.

> What God speaks He performs, He does not change His mind.

The child has nothing to say about this circumcision, but it is administered in any case. And again, when it is, the results are permanent. For whatever reason, the child may grow up not being all that happy about being Jewish. And yet, he cannot change that circumcision. He even may run away from home. He may go off into the proverbial "far country." But wherever he goes, the mark of who he is goes with him. It is a sign of the fact, that when God establishes a covenant, it is established forever.

God's Covenant Is Gracious

God's promises all are undeserved. With respect to the specific covenantal promises given to Abraham, Moses writes: "It was not because you were more in number than any other people that the Lord set his love on you and chose you, for you were the fewest of all peoples, but it is because the Lord loves and is keeping the oath that he swore to your fathers, that the Lord has brought you out with a mighty hand and redeemed you from the house of slavery..." (Deuteronomy 7:7, 8). And it is no different for any of us in this day of God's grace. When He comes to us, we have done nothing to deserve His promises. God nevertheless makes them. He does so simply because it pleases Him to do it. He does so because His promises are saturated with total, unmerited favor. He acts, "...for the sake of his name."

> *God's promises all are undeserved.*

When God acts, His saving grace is more costly to Him than our poor intellect can ever fathom. In terms of God's covenantal promise to Abraham, it is *ratified* by a ceremony requiring the shedding of blood. In Genesis 15, God ratifies the terms of His covenantal agreement by the shedding of the blood of dismantled parts of slain animals. In Genesis 17, it is the blood shed in circumcision that is a reminder of covenantal relationship.

> *The ultimate fulfillment of the Abrahamic covenant being ratified is seen in the shedding of our Savior's blood.*

The ultimate fulfillment of the Abrahamic covenant being ratified is seen in the shedding of our Savior's blood. It is why Hebrews refers to the shed blood of Jesus on Calvary's cross as "the blood of the everlasting covenant." It also is why we today sing:

There is a fountain filled with blood.

Drawn from Immanuel's veins.

And sinners plunged beneath that flood lose all their guilty stains.

The New Covenant Prophesied by Jeremiah Is the Fulfillment of the Old Covenant Announced to Abraham

For it is not possible that the blood of bulls and goats should take away sins. †Hebrews 10:4

Therefore he is the mediator of a new covenant, so that those who are called may receive the promised eternal inheritance, since a death has occurred that redeems them from the transgressions committed under the first covenant. †Hebrews 9:15

But you have come to Mount Zion and to the city of the living God, the heavenly Jerusalem... and to the assembly of the firstborn who are enrolled in heaven... and to Jesus, the mediator of a new covenant, and to the sprinkled blood that speaks a better word than the blood of Abel. †Hebrews 12:22-24

THE BOOK OF HEBREWS CLARIFIES the nature of that "new covenant" mentioned by Jeremiah. It is *"new,"* not in the sense that it is *totally different*. It is *"new"* in the sense that it is the perfected expression of the *"old"* covenantal commitment to Abraham.

"Jesus," says the writer of Hebrews, is "the mediator of a better covenant which was established upon better promises." Again, these "better promises" are not intrinsically *different*. However they *are* "better" with respect to the promised access to God, with respect to God's abundant grace that is communicated, with respect to the degree of intimacy of fellowship that is promised.

The sacrifice to be made is better. The High Priest who carries out the sacrifice is better. The sanctuary into which the

High Priest enters is better. The destination prepared for the covenant people is better.

Even today, when we describe something as *"new,"* we are not necessarily saying it is *totally different*. In one sense a Lamborghini sports car is not the same car as the Model T Ford. But the two cars, although very different, do operate on similar principles. There is an internal combustion engine, driving cylinders up and down, consequently turning a crankshaft connected to gears within an axle, propelling the wheels of both cars, either forward or backward.

> *When we describe something as "new" we are not necessarily saying it is totally different.*

In a somewhat similar manner, Jeremiah's *"new covenant"* will operate in an unsurpassed way to bring God's covenantal promise announced to Abraham to a glorious and perfected realization. The promised commitment, "I will be their God and they shall be my people" will take on a clearer, more personal dimension in this New Testament dispensation.

As was mentioned, no longer do we look for God through Old Testament "types" and "symbols." These are described as "shadows" of the One who is to come. We no longer need these Levitical types and shadows of the Old Testament. We now see Jesus, the Messenger of the covenant, face to face (John 1:14).

> *No longer do we look for God through Old Testament "types" and "symbols".*

We no longer need "wave offerings," "heave offerings," "grain offerings" and "sin offerings". We no longer need the blood of bulls as a symbol of taking away sins. The *"new"* has come! We now "Behold the Lamb of God, who takes away the sin of the world." We gaze upon His finished work on Calvary.

The *new covenant* also is better than the *old* in that the Mediator no longer is confined to the nation of Israel. The knowledge of the Lord now fully comes to all nations. Jesus declares, "All shall know me, from the least to the greatest" (Hebrews 8:11). Jesus is not simply interested in Middle Eastern real estate. He never was! In fact, it is why He issued His "Great Commission": "Go therefore, and teach *all nations*."

The *new* is superior to the *old*, in that the Holy Spirit now is poured forth in greater abundance upon the New Testament people of God. In fact, the Holy Spirit accomplishes the very prophecy of Jeremiah 3:2: "I will put my laws into their minds and write them in their hearts." The Holy Spirit establishes a new bond of greater, more vital fellowship with the promised Savior. The Holy Spirit does even more. He causes the "fruit of the Spirit" to abound in believers' lives. He causes them to become a Kingdom of kings and priests to their God. No wonder then, that the writer of Hebrews states: "If that first covenant had been faultless there would have been no occasion to look for a second" (Hebrews 8:7).

> *The New Covenant expands the old covenant promise. It fulfills the old covenant promise. It perfects the old covenant promise.*

So then, the New Covenant *expands* the old covenant promise. It *fulfills* the old covenant promise. It *perfects* the old covenant promise. But at the same time it must be repeated that it is "the blood of the *everlasting* covenant that equips us with everything good, that we may do God's will" (Hebrews 13:20,21). It is because of this "blood of the everlasting covenant," that we experience today, the joy of singing:

A debtor to mercy alone
Of covenant mercy I sing!
Nor fear with Thy righteousness on
My person and offering to bring.

Throughout the entire Bible there is but one central message. It is a message speaking of salvation by a Redeemer. It *connects* the many other messages of Scripture. It is the very message that confirms God's *covenant of saving grace*, first announced to Abraham. God's covenant promise expresses His plan to save man from the just consequences of his sin. This covenantal saving grace is "...God's finger on man's shoulder." It finds its clearest expressions and summary in those familiar words of Jesus: "God so loved the word that he gave His only begotten Son, that whosoever believeth in Him should not perish, but have everlasting life" (John 3:16).

FOOD FOR THOUGHT

"The concept of covenant, which provides the structure or framework of redemptive history and of the whole scope of theology, is vitally important. It provides the content within which God reveals himself to us, ministers to us, and acts to redeem us… The language and concept of covenant pervades redemptive history and the Bible… To understand Jesus and his redeeming work, we must first understand the covenantal structure in which God promised a Savior for a lost and fallen race… The history of redemption did not begin with the birth of Jesus. In a sense Jesus' birth was the culmination of all the promises that God had made over the centuries." QUOTES #20

QUESTIONS FOR FEEDBACK

❶ What does it mean when scripture says God is jealous? How does this trait relate to the Covenant he makes with Abraham?

❷ When someone points to the fact that God's Covenant with Abraham was sovereignly imposed, what do they mean?

❸ What is meant by the statement: There is only one covenant of saving grace between God and man in all dispensations?

❹ If a person considers the Ten Commandments to be morally binding on today's believer, is it legitimate to describe such a person as a "legalist"? If so, why? If not, why not?

❺ What seals or secures God's covenant promise to Abraham?

❻ How does the New Covenant supersede or fulfill the Old Covenant?

GOD'S FINGER ON MAN'S SHOULDER

CHAPTER 8

DOING AS WE PLEASE

"When we examine the question of free will… we are pressured by the massive impact that secular views of free will have had on our thinking. If there is any place where secular humanism has undermined a biblical view of human nature, it's with respect to the idea of free will. The prevailing view of free will in the secular culture is that human beings are able to make choices, without being encumbered by sin. On this view, our wills have no predisposition either toward evil or toward righteousness, but remain in a neutral state from birth." **QUOTES #21**

"MAINE'S GROWING EVANGELICAL CHURCHES" IS the title of a recent article in the *Downeast* magazine. The author states that although the state of Maine ranks among the most secular states in the nation, its evangelical churches are experiencing impressive numerical growth, a phenomenon that has gone unnoticed in the mainstream media.

Toward the end of this fascinating story an evangelical pastor from the city of Bangor was interviewed. When asked about the current hot topic in evangelicalism, it was reported that his voice grew lively. He responded: "*Calvinism* and the limits of God's power in people's lives. What is the extent of man's free will versus God's sovereignty."

The pastor's answer is not surprising. What is particularly fascinating about his comment is this: whenever the subject of free will is debated, it frequently is assumed that those who are labeled as "Calvinists" teach that people do not have an unrestrained free will. It is an assumption that goes counter to reality. In fact, those referred to as "Calvinists" actually agree that people certainly DO have a free will. People make choices every day. They are "free agents." However such daily choices are made within the context of who people are.

> People certainly do have a free will. People make choices every day. They are "free agents." However, such daily choices are made within the context of who people are.

Our Choices Reflect Who We Are

Many are the plans in a man's heart, but it is the Lord's purpose that prevails. †Proverbs 19:21

The mind that is set on the flesh is hostile to God, for it does not submit to God's law, indeed, it cannot. †Romans 8:7

WHEN IT COMES TO UNDERSTANDING who we are, psychologists often stress the importance of understanding one's personality profile. They also remind folks to be careful not to answer personality tests in such a way that they select responses they think are more acceptable because they have an image in their mind of what might be a proper answer. If such caution is not exercised, the results can be damaging, even disastrous. Picking the wrong personality type can be like putting diesel fuel into a car that takes regular gasoline. Not only will the wrong fuel not work properly; worse yet, it will damage the car's engine.

> *Because Adam sinned, he forfeited the possibility of a perfect freedom, and therefore a perfect righteousness for all those whom he represented.*

What is true psychologically is even truer spiritually. In answering the question: Who am I? The Apostle Paul paints a picture of man's solidarity with Adam. The message of Romans 5 emphasizes a universal reign of spiritual and physical death that is the consequence of one man's disobedience.

What the Bible teaches is bold and far-reaching. Because Adam sinned, he forfeited the possibility of a perfect freedom, and therefore a perfect righteousness for all those whom he represented. "Sin came into the world through one man and death (both physical and spiritual) through sin, and so death spread to *all* men because *all* sinned ...Because of one man's trespass death reigned through that one man" (Romans 5:12, 17).

> *Our responses are the direct consequence of who we are.*

That message is a whole lot more than just abstract theology. It impacts the daily decisions we all make. Our responses are the direct consequence of who we are. We first envision what we believe is advantageous to us. We then express these convictions in the choices we make.

No one is forcing such desires upon us. We simply do what we please to do. At times our actions may be spontaneous. They may even be enjoyable. But whether deliberate or spontaneous, whether painful or pleasant, no one is imposing those decisions upon us. We are the ones who determine our course of action. We are the ones who exercise a free will.

But it is important that we ask another question. Is this free will always *liberating*? Does our free will always result in what might be described as our ultimate well being? The answer is: not really! It would be naive to think otherwise.

In the words of Aldous Huxley, "A man's worst difficulties begin when he is able to do what he likes." In terms of people's freedom to make choices, it cannot be denied that individuals *do* have such freedom. However, we need to address a more penetrating issue. In every dimension of life the kind of freedom that helps and does not hurt always will involve the *ability* to do what is right. A truly liberating freedom says that we are free to obey those laws that have been established for our welfare and happiness. If we are not willingly obedient to such recognized laws, principles, and procedures, the consequences are never pleasant.

> A true liberating freedom says that we are free to obey those laws that have been established for our welfare and happiness.

For example, try sitting down at a piano and just banging away on any of the keys indiscriminatingly. Jokingly, we may announce that we are playing the piano. But everyone who hears will know we are merely making noise. Why? Because it is a fundamental fact of life: it takes obedience to the accepted laws of music to play even the most basic tune. There is a logical structure to those notes on the page.

In living our lives, if we are to experience a freedom that is liberating, something basic must happen. We must participate in the discipline of conforming to the God-ordained principles of such liberated living. We must live according to the laws of God's Word.

Having said this, we come back to that basic question: do we make free will choices every day of our lives? Yes, we do. It is obvious that we do. But the more important question to ask is this: do we experience a truly liberating freedom in the making of these choices? The answer to that question comes down to how a person defines the concept of "true freedom."

With respect to unsaved people having a liberated freedom to "choose Jesus," there is yet another fundamental issue that must be confronted. The issue is this: what do those who are described in Scripture as "...dead in trespasses and sins" truly desire in life? Scripture teaches that the answer to that question will bring an individual back to the message of Genesis 3.

Choices Reflect Free Will Before and After Events of Genesis 3

Can the Ethiopian change his skin or the leopard his spots? Then can you also do good who are accustomed to do evil? † **Jeremiah 134:23**

The natural person does not accept the things of the spirit of God, for they are folly to him, and he is not able to understand them because they are spiritually discerned. † **I Corinthians 2:14**

No one can come to me unless the Father who sent me draws him. † **John 6:44**

IT WOULD BE SAFE TO say that numerous people struggle with the Bible's message relative to the paralyzing consequences of Adam's fall into sin. Many would, in fact, reject such teaching. Unfortunately, all too many believers, when thinking about man's free will, also fail to recognize the effects of Adam's sin upon the human race. In particular, they seem to assume that man does not have a bent from birth to doing evil.

Yet, after David's tragic transgression against Bathsheba and her husband, what does he say in Psalm 51:5? He affirms that he has not come into this world as an innocent human being. "In sin did my mother conceive me." Such a statement is true of all mankind. Just like King David, we all come into this world in a state of moral deformity. Our condition is pervasive. It is irrational. It is crippling.

> We all come into this world in a state of moral deformity, Our condition is pervasive. It is irrational. It is crippling.

From the moment we take our first breath, we want, what we want, when we want it. It's just another way of saying that our hearts are inclined toward sin. What is in our hearts becomes the root source of all the actions of our lives. The Bible teaches that all mankind has a predisposition toward evil, not toward good. People do not come into this world as "blank slates." They do not enter life in a neutral state.

They are impacted by Adam's fall. The consequences are profound. They are crippling. Complicated. Condemning. No longer can such choices be described as "righteous." Instead, they are preferences that are self-serving. There is an habitual attraction to do what pleases man, not what pleases God. It is because decisions cannot be detached from the one making the decision.

> We exercise an unrelenting willingness to do the very things that are contrary to God's expressed will for our lives.

Spiritually speaking, the answer to the question: "who are we?" is not a happy one. We are a people with a predisposition inherited from the federal head of the human race. As a consequence, like Adam, we exercise an unrelenting willingness to do the very things that are contrary to God's expressed will for our lives.

The Bible puts it quite forcefully: we do not "...accept the things of the spirit of God for they are folly to us." We are not even able to understand "...the things of the spirit of God." Why not? Because these things "...are spiritually discerned" (I Corinthians 2:14). The prophet Jeremiah expresses a similar condemning commentary: "Can the Ethiopian change his skin or the leopard change his spots?" Obviously they cannot! And neither, writes Jeremiah, can those individuals "...do good who are accustomed to do evil" (Jeremiah 13:23).

> *The things God desires for His creatures are the very things which are folly to the unbeliever.*

The things God desires for His creatures are the very things which are folly to the unbeliever. No amount of will power can change that fact. The leopard doesn't change his spots. Decisions made cannot be detached from who we are.

In the physical realm, no one can change the nature of their capabilities. People cannot walk on water, nor can they energetically flap their arms and begin to fly. And neither can those who are spiritually dead somehow exercise their wills in such a fashion that they become a people they are not.

> *When Adam made the conscious choice to do what God had commanded him not to do, both he and we lost the kind of freedom to do that which truly liberates.*

Once more we come back to that most basic question: "who are we?" The answer, says Romans 5, is this: we have inherited Adam's fallen nature. We all "...have sinned and come short of the glory of God." What happened to the progenitor of the human race has been passed on to us.

When Adam made the conscious choice to do what God had commanded him not to do, both he and we lost the kind of freedom to do that which truly liberates. What was lost is the capacity to do what is well pleasing in the sight of God. It comes down to this: sin obscured Adam's judgment. Sin now has dominion over our judgment.

Ephesians 2 describes this state as "spiritual death." Romans 5 puts it this way: "Just as sin came into the world through one man (Adam), and death through sin... so death spread to all men because all sinned." Romans 5 goes on to say: "Because of one man's trespass (Adam's trespass), death reigned through that one man." It is a commentary that concludes with four unrelenting words: "Sin reigned in death" (Romans 5:12-21).

Such are the ravages of sin! "A man's worst difficulties begin when he is able to do as he likes."(Aldous Huxley) Obviously then, we do have a free will to make choices. However, these choices inevitably will be the consequence of our fallen nature. Our contaminated nature. Our self-serving nature. It is why Jesus announced: "No one can come to me unless the Father who sent me draws him" (John 6:44).

> *If man's heart of stone does not become a heart of flesh, he will continue to be unresponsive to God's gracious offer of salvation.*

The Savior is reminding folks that the heart of fallen man is not tender and responsive to the gospel message. Rather, the heart of man is hard. It is, says Scripture, "a heart of stone!" As such, it will not and cannot accept God's invitation to experience forgiveness and life abundant, unless a sovereign and regenerating work of God's grace takes place. Man's heart of stone must become a heart of flesh. The message of John 6 is clear: if man's heart of stone does not become a heart of flesh, he will continue to be unresponsive to God's gracious offer of salvation.

Is man free? Oh, yes! But what also is true is this: the freedom of man's fallen nature will not allow him to do what God wants. The freedom of man's fallen nature will not allow him to choose that which is pleasing in the sight of a holy God.

The Holy Spirit Must Quicken Dead Minds, Hearts, and Wills

I will give you a new heart, and a new spirit I will put within you. And I will remove the heart of stone from your flesh and give you a heart of flesh. And I will put my spirit within you, and cause you to walk in my statutes... †Ezekiel 36:26, 27

...everyone who is born of God does not keep on sinning. †I John 5:18

ONCE MORE, IT IS IMPERATIVE to come back to the words of Jesus: "No one can come to me unless it has been granted to him by my Father." The assertion Jesus makes is of far reaching consequences. "No one can come" only can mean one thing: *nobody can*!

By way of illustration, I well remember watching a captivating TV movie in which an elementary age schoolboy who recently had immigrated to the United States raised his hand to ask his teacher a question; "*Can* I go to the bathroom?" The teacher answered: "You *can* but you *may* not."

The boy was totally confused. He had no idea whether his teacher was saying, "Yes, you can," or if she was saying, "No, you may not." In his confusion, he missed the teacher's point. She was trying to communicate that his choice of the word "*can*" had to do with his *ability*. What

> John 6:44 is telling us that without a prior work of the Holy Spirit, fallen man does not have the ability to turn to Jesus. "No one can come to me unless it has been granted to him."

he should have said was, "*May* I go to the bathroom?" Why? Because the word "*may*" has to do with *permission*.

John 6:44 is telling us that without a prior work of the Holy Spirit, fallen man does not have the ability to turn to Jesus. "No one can come to me unless it has been *granted* to him." In other words, no one is *able*! It is precisely why C. S. Lewis, in describing his conversion experience, wrote, "I was the *object* rather than the *subject* in this affair. I was decided upon."

As with C. S. Lewis, so it is with every follower of Jesus. The Holy Spirit must take the initiative, creating within individuals a desire for Jesus, and creating an ability to come to Jesus.

There is yet another telling dimension incorporated in the words of John 6:44. When Jesus used the expression, "...can come," He was using the very same word that also can be found in Acts 16:19. It is a word that in the book of Acts is saying that the men of Philippi literally "dragged" Paul and Silas before the authorities. In John 6:44, Jesus was being equally graphic: no man can come to me unless the Father, in effect, "drags" him to come.

> *The sinner is literally compelled by the Holy Spirit to come to the Savior.*

In Acts 16:19, officials in the city of Philippi did not somehow encourage or entice Paul and Silas to come before the legal authorities. And in John 6:44, Jesus is saying much the same thing. He is saying that when the Holy Spirit invades a sinner's life, what is experienced is not some protracted process of pleading and persuasion. The sinner is literally *compelled* by the Holy Spirit to come to the Savior.

In all areas of life, including the area of man's free will, we either have a God-centered understanding of who we are, or we have a man-centered understanding of who we are. It was because King David had a compelling awareness of this very fact that he also penned these words: "Blessed is the one *you choose* and bring near, to dwell in your courts" (Psalm 65:4).

FOOD FOR THOUGHT

"Every Christian will have either a God-centered or a man-centered theology... There simply is no such thing as a will which is detached from and totally independent of the person making the choice... Men choose the things they do because as the complex, finite person that they are, and the Bible informs us that men are not only finite but are now also sinners, who by nature cannot bring forth good fruit (Matt. 7:18) ...and by nature cannot come to Christ (John 6:44, 45, 65). In order to do any of these things they must receive powerful aid coming to them... It is an exceedingly dangerous approach to base any doctrine on human intuition rather than on God's authoritative Word." QUOTES #22

QUESTIONS FOR FEEDBACK

1. When it comes to an individual's unsaved, spiritual condition, how dead is dead?

2. What is it that determines a person's will?

3. Since man is able to do either good or evil, why does Genesis 6:5 say that "every imagination of the thoughts of his heart is only evil continually?"

4. In John 8:34-36, what issues does Jesus force people to confront?

5. In Romans 8:5-8, what does the apostle say about the option people have in living their lives?

6. If regeneration precedes everything in salvation, does this mean the sinner is not responsible for refusing to believe the gospel?

DOING AS WE PLEASE

CHAPTER 9

ONE CALL THAT CHANGES ALL

"The question is: Why do some accept and others reject this offer of eternal life? The answer is that it is contrary to the will and desire of man to accept it, until ...their basic nature is changed." QUOTES #23

IN EVERYDAY LIFE, EFFICIENCY AND effectiveness can often function as mutually exclusive realities. Even our use of technologies such as smart phones, text messaging, and e-mails may not fully correct the problem. What is accomplished because of such technologies may be done with greater speed but not necessarily with greater effectiveness. We may, in fact, be doing the wrong things. For this reason, management gurus emphasize that a person ought to strive to be *efficiently effective*.

It is an objective that is particularly relevant in terms of man's salvation. Most assuredly, the God of the Bible is efficiently effective. Romans 8:30 puts it this way: "Those whom God predestined he also called and those he called he also justified and those he justified he also glorified."

> When God's sovereign, saving grace invades a life, it is efficiently effective.

Romans 8 is saying this: when God's sovereign, saving grace invades a life, it is *efficiently effective*. Into that blessed life is infused the transforming power of the Holy Spirit. When this converting power of the Holy Spirit impacts a life, He also inverts the direction of that life. He alters the direction so totally that each individual becomes all God intends for them to become.

God's Effectual Call is Not the Same As His General Call

Many are called but few are chosen. †**Matthew 22:14**

Then Jesus, deeply moved came to the tomb... He cried out with a loud voice, 'Lazarus, come out.' The man who had died came out...
†**John 11:38-44**

To this God called you through our gospel, so that you may obtain the glory of our Lord Jesus Christ. †**II Thessalonians 2:14**

IN EVERYDAY LIFE, NOT ALL who hear God's gospel message evidence a positive response to the "good news." They have ears to hear, but they do not truly hear in a saving way. Jesus taught that they do not hear in a saving way because, "...no one knows the Father except the Son and anyone to whom the Son chooses to reveal him" (Matthew 11:27).

> *Spiritually speaking, individuals "come alive" because they have been quickened by the Holy Spirit*

To all who "have ears to hear," Jesus is saying this: It is not because of man's initiative that man experiences God's saving grace. Rather, salvation becomes a reality because of God's *effectual calling*.

Spiritually speaking, individuals *"come alive"* because they have been quickened by the Holy Spirit. They experience much more than a general call from God. They experience an effectual call. Such an effective call causes those who truly "hear" also to "taste and see that the Lord is good." An effectual call from God causes them to become "new creatures in Christ Jesus."

It is precisely this matter of God's "effectual call" that is being addressed in Matthew 22. In the parable of the wedding feast, Jesus describes a certain king who is about to honor his soon to be married son. A general invitation went out to all: come to my son's wedding feast. But the parable does not end with this general invitation. Jesus puts it this way:

> "When the king came in to look at the guests, he saw there was a man who had no wedding garment... How did you get in here without a wedding garment? And the man was speechless... Bind him hand and foot and cast him into utter darkness... *for many are called but few are chosen.*"

The point of Jesus' teaching is a sobering one. It is not sufficient simply to hear a *general call* to come to the marriage feast. Something indispensable is demanded of all legitimate participants at this banquet. They must be clothed in wedding garments provided by the king. If they are not, they disobey the king. They dishonor the king.

As with all of Jesus' parables, there is an important spiritual application. Jesus is saying that those who attend the "Marriage Supper of the Lamb" will be those who not only hear a general call to the "Wedding Feast," they also are those who are clothed in garments of righteousness which are provided by the king. In other words, they are trusting in the righteousness of the King's Son to cover their spiritual nakedness. It is a critically important distinction. And because it is, the final words of the parable are both solemn and severe: "Many are called but few are chosen." Jesus is letting everyone know that simply hearing the general call of the gospel does not necessarily result in salvation.

> Doing the will of God is not something that man through his own natural inclinations chooses.

It is this same reality that the apostle Paul has in mind as he admonishes Timothy to "Take hold of the eternal life to which you were called" (I Timothy 6:12). The apostle is emphasizing a particular kind of call that Timothy has received. It is an effectual call of God. It is a saving call from God.

It is this same "effectual call" that Paul again has in mind in II Timothy 1:9. We are "...saved and called to a holy calling, not because of our works but because of his own purpose and grace, which he gave us in Christ Jesus."

The message of Scripture is one that says: Doing the will of God is not something that man through his own natural inclinations chooses. Individuals may hear a "general call" in the proclamation of the Gospel, but eternal life is a destination to which God must call His chosen children. It is only God who "effectually calls." It is only God who brings about new life. It is life that truly originates from above.

Effectual calling carries with it the kind of *re-creative* power so impressively demonstrated in the raising of Lazarus from the grave.

Brain waves within his dead body return. His heart beat returns. When Jesus calls out, "Lazarus, come forth!" in an instant this man comes alive. Blood circulation returns. Lazarus walks out of His tomb of death. He is utterly changed by the effectual call of Jesus.

> *Effectual calling carries with it the kind of re-creative power so impressively demonstrated in the raising of Lazarus from the grave.*

Why is such effectual calling necessary? It is because of what Ephesians 2 teaches. Every person coming into this world is just as dead spiritually as Lazarus was dead physically. All are "dead in trespasses and sins." They walk through life "...following the course of this world." By nature, all are "children of wrath, like the rest of mankind."

But when the Holy Spirit *effectually calls*, "Come forth," something extreme happens. Men and women come out of their tomb of spiritual death. They come forth to new life. It is a new and different quality of life. Ephesians 2:4 describes it this way: "God who is rich in mercy" demonstrates his "...great love with which he loved us, even when we were dead in our trespasses."

When God in mercy effectually calls individuals to Himself, it is an *efficiently effective* call from heaven's high throne. Because of such a supernatural calling, God accomplishes in His chosen children precisely what He has ordained for them. His chosen

> *Because of such a supernatural calling, God accomplishes in His chosen children precisely what He has ordained for them.*

children will know the joy of sins forgiven. They also will participate in God's ongoing work of sanctification. Likewise, they will experience what it means to suffer for the Savior. They will experience what it means to be called to a new and radical pattern of living, one in which their Savior "...also suffered, leaving them an example, that they should follow in his steps" (I Peter 2:21).

Effectual Calling and the Message of John 3

That which is born of the flesh is flesh and that which is born of the Spirit is spirit. Do not marvel that I said unto you, you must be born again. †John 3:6, 7

IN THE POIGNANT NARRATIVE OF John 3, a deeply religious man named Nicodemus comes to Jesus. He is a respected spiritual leader in Israel. When he comes to Jesus, he is more than simply curious. He is conflicted.

The message and the miracles of the Rabbi from Nazareth have created all kinds of questions. They are not inconsequential questions.

Nicodemus comes to Jesus by night. It is not simply because the man desires privacy. His reasons for coming at night are far deeper than that. He is determined to have Jesus all to himself. And why not? The amazing signs and wonders Nicodemus has witnessed have made an indelible impact. They also have created lots of questions.

The kingdom of God does not and cannot begin with fallen, sinful man. The kingdom of God must begin with a holy, yet compassionate God.

This special leader in Israel struggles to reconcile what he has seen and heard with what he has been taught all his life. Yet, in spite of such conflicted thoughts and feelings, he nevertheless is convinced: Jesus is uniquely sent from God. "Rabbi, we know that you are a teacher from God, for no one can do these signs that you do unless God is with him."

Quite a compliment! But it elicits no response from Jesus. The necessary action that overshadows everything else is this: how does a man enter the kingdom of God? So the Savior "jumps right in." He wants Nicodemus to confront a matter of preeminent importance. The kingdom of God does not and cannot begin with fallen, sinful man. The kingdom of God must begin with a holy, yet compassionate God.

> *If this regenerating work of the Holy Spirit does not happen, there is no entrance into the kingdom of God.*

Our Savior, therefore, "cuts to the chase." Time cannot be wasted in "pleasantries." Immediately Jesus describes to this searching soul a quality of life whose origin is in heaven, not on earth. It is a dimension of life created by the power of the Holy Spirit. If this regenerating work of the Holy Spirit does not happen, there is no entrance into the kingdom of God.

> *Preeminently, it is all about what God first must do in the human heart.*

Nicodemus hears the words, yet he does not "get it." He is utterly perplexed. The man may be a spiritual leader in Israel, but he has no idea what Jesus is talking about. "Truly, truly I say to you unless one is born of water, even the Spirit, he cannot enter the kingdom of God. That which is born of the flesh is flesh and that which is born of the Spirit is spirit. Do not marvel that I said to you, you must be born again."

What Jesus is saying is this: the kingdom of God has little to do with the fact that this man has experienced a positive response to the message and miracles of the Master. It has little to do with the fact that Nicodemus is considered by many to be a "man of faith." In fact, it does not even relate to how much this man may be thinking about whether or not he should choose to follow Jesus.

It all comes back to one thing, says Jesus. Preeminently, it is all about what God *first* must do in the human heart. First, you must be "born from above." First you must be "born again." Where there is no life, Nicodemus, God must create life.

Is this work of the Holy Spirit a mystery? Oh yes! But, it remains the number one issue. Unless and until a man is "...born from above, he cannot enter the kingdom of God." It is what *effectual calling* is all about. It also is what the hymn writer had in mind when he penned these perceptive words:

> I sought the Lord and afterward I knew
> > He moved my soul to seek Him seeking me.
> It was not I that found, O Savior true,
> > No, I was found of Thee.
>
> —George W. Chadwick

FOOD FOR THOUGHT

"Regeneration is the beginning of all saving grace in us, and all saving grace in exercise on our part proceeds from the fountain of regeneration. We are not born again by faith or repentance or conversion; we repent and believe because we have been regenerated."

QUOTES #24

QUESTIONS FOR RESPONSE

1. To what two classes of men does the gospel come? Why do they react differently to the free offer of salvation?

2. Looking at John 3:1-8, describe the Holy Spirit's work of regeneration?

3. To what extent may a person be affected by the general call of the gospel, without true conversion? Why do these people fail to come to Christ? Is this the fault of God? Explain.

4. According to Romans 8:28-30, what are the steps involved in a person's coming to saving faith in Christ?

5. What does Titus 3:4-7 say about God's character? About his work in us? How does this promote humility and gratitude?

6. How did the Holy Spirit draw you to Christ? What influences did he use that you can only appreciate now as you look back on your conversion?

CHAPTER 10

A DECLARATION OF DEPENDENCE

"We were created for intimate fellowship with God and for freedom, but we have disgraced ourselves by unfaithfulness... Jesus, our faithful Bridegroom and lover, entered the market-place to buy us back. He bid his own blood. There is no higher bid than that and we become his. He reclothed us, not in the wretched rags of our old unrighteousness, but in his new robes of righteousness." **QUOTES #25**

The Message of Salvation by Grace Alone

LARGELY FORGOTTEN TODAY, GEORGE WHITFIELD probably was the most famous religious figure of the eighteenth century. Newspapers called this man the "marvel of the age." In his lifetime he preached more than 18,000 gospel messages to as many as ten million people. Before his seven tours of the American colonies were complete, virtually every man, woman and child had heard at least one of Whitfield's gospel presentations. So pervasive was this man's impact upon the thirteen British colonies, he has been described quite justly as America's first cultural hero. From north to south, from Boston to Charleston, it is doubtful any man was as well known as George Whitfield.

He is one of only three men credited with having ignited the spiritual revival often described as The Great Awakening. There can be no doubt, Whitfield's reintroduction of the gospel message of justification by faith alone, through grace alone, because of the sacrifice of Christ alone, became one of the most formative events in early American history.

His very last open air sermon was on a favorite, often repeated theme: How do those who are unrighteous, stand before the justice of a righteous, holy God. In the words of Psalm 130:3: "If you, O Lord, should mark iniquities, O Lord, who could stand?"

Whitfield delivered this message simply titled: "Faith and Works" in the open fields of Exeter, New Hampshire, to tens of thousands of people, while standing atop a large barrel. Looking to heaven, he prayed: "Lord Jesus, I am weary in Thy work, but not of Thy work. If I have not yet finished my course, let me go and speak for Thee once more in the fields, seal Thy truth, and come and die."

Undeniably, Whitfield was given strength for this, his last sermon to a mass audience of thousands. One of those in attendance passed along this story to a local newspaper. "He was speaking of the inefficiency of works to merit salvation. Suddenly he cried out in a tone of thunder, 'Works! Works! A man gets to heaven by works! I would as soon think of climbing to the moon on a rope of sand.'"

The very next morning George Whitfield died in Newburyport, Massachusetts, about thirty miles south of Exeter. He was just fifty-six years old when he laid down his life in defense of a gospel message he loved dearly: justification by faith alone. Even one of this nation's founding fathers, Benjamin Franklin, wrote that he had "...never heard and never witnessed anything like what he heard and witnessed in the outdoor preaching of George Whitfield."

I mention this true story because this is a day when people are uncomfortable with Whitfield's message. Today they do not want to hear about a holy God. Or sinful man. Or the judgment seat of God. Whitfield may have sparked America's Great Awakening, but at the site of his final message in Exeter, New Hampshire, all you will see today is a small granite marker, standing just off ground level with one word, "*Whitfield*" chiseled into the granite. That's all! People pass by. They do not notice. They do not care. And they certainly do not want to be reminded of that transforming message preached throughout our nation's original colonies.

> *God judges according to an unwavering standard of perfect righteousness...*

The indifference of man, however, does not change God's message. He still judges human deeds. God judges according to an unwavering standard of perfect righteousness. Such knowledge is intimidating. It is frightening.

"The wrath of God," wrote Jonathan Edwards, "is like great waters that are dammed for the present. They increase more and more and rise higher and higher until an outlet is given. The longer the stream is stopped, the more rapid and mighty is its course when once it is let loose."

But there also "...is forgiveness, that God may be feared," wrote the Psalmist. It is a forgiveness that does not compromise God's holiness. It is a forgiveness that most certainly does punish sin. It is what *justification* is all about.

How God Justifies sinners

Jesus... gave himself for our sins... according to the will of our God and Father. †Galatians 1:14

I have been crucified with Christ... and the life I now live in the flesh I live by faith in the Son of God, who loved me, and gave himself for me. †Galatians 2:20

Christ redeemed us from the curse of the law, by becoming a curse for us. For it is written, 'cursed is everyone who is hanged on a tree.'
†Galatians 3:13

...Christ loved us and gave himself for us, a fragrant offering and sacrifice to God. †Ephesians 5:2

Who gave himself a ransom for all... †I Timothy 2:6

ON THE CROSS OF CALVARY Jesus assumed our identity. He endured the judgment of God due to our sins. He suffered as a substitute for His "called out" people. Jesus suffered for the detestable and damning record of our sins. It was a seemingly endless list of sin. They were our sins and they were nailed to Calvary's cross.

> *Jesus suffered for the detestable and damning record of our sins*

The spotless Lamb of God had committed no sin, and yet, Scripture says, "He bore our sins in His own body on the tree." It is "...by His wounds we have been healed" (I Peter 2:24). It is an overwhelming reality that moved Horatius Bonar to write:

> Not what my hands have done
> > Can save my guilty soul;
> Not what my toiling flesh has borne
> > Can make my spirit whole.
> Thy work alone, O Christ,
> > Can ease this weight of sin;
> Thy blood alone, O Lamb of God,
> > Can give me peace within.

Justification comes down to this: ours is a total lack of merit. Ours is a desperate need for God's grace. "By the deeds of the law, no flesh will be justified in God's sight" (Romans 3:20). God must give to man what he never can hope to achieve on his own. The theological term for such a transaction is *imputation*. God credits a righteousness to man that he never can earn. It is this that the writer of Colossians 1:19-22 has in mind. Jesus has "...made peace by the blood of His cross. And you, who once were alienated and hostile in mind, doing evil deeds, He has now reconciled... by His death, in order to present you holy and blameless and above reproach before Him." Such double imputation is the sinner's only hope before a holy God. God looks upon those justified by grace through faith in His Son and He sees Jesus. They are "hid with God in Christ."

> God looks upon those justified by grace through faith in His Son and he sees Jesus. They are "hid with God in Christ."

"In Christ Jesus, you are all sons of God, through faith. For as many of you as were baptized have put on Christ" (Galatians 3:26,27). "In him we have redemption through His blood, the forgiveness of our trespasses, according to the riches of his grace... God being rich in mercy, because of the great love with which he loved us... made us alive together with Christ...

now in Christ Jesus you who once were far off have been brought near by the blood of Christ" (Ephesians 1:7; 2:4, 5, 13).

If we look through a piece of red glass, everything appears as red. If we look through a piece of blue glass, everything appears as blue. And those with a truly penitent, believing faith in the finished work of Christ for them are seen as being "in Christ Jesus." They are seen in all the white holiness of God's Son. Their vile sins have been imputed to the Son. What also is true is this: the perfect righteousness of the Son has been imputed to them.

> *God must give to man what he never can hope to achieve on his own. The theological term for such a transaction is imputation. God credits a righteousness to man that he never can earn.*

At Calvary Jesus paid a debt He did not owe. The Savior did this because His chosen sons and daughters owed a debt they could not pay. The transfer that took place at the cross was nothing less than a staggering *double transfer*. It overwhelmed the heart of Horatius Bonar. He wrote:

> I lay my sins on Jesus the spotless Lamb of God
> He bears them all and frees us, from the accursed load.
> I bring my guilt to Jesus, to wash my crimson stains
> White in His blood most precious 'til not a spot remains.

Faith Is the Only Condition to Receive an Undeserved Righteousness

"To the one who does not work but trusts him who justifies the ungodly, his faith is counted as righteousness." †**Romans 4:5**

"Since we have been justified by faith, we have peace with God through our Lord Jesus Christ." †**Romans 5:1**

"We also have believed in Christ Jesus, in order to be justified by faith in Christ, and not by works of the law, because by works of the law no one will be justified." †Galatians 2:16

"For by grace you have been saved through faith, and this is not your own doing; it is the gift of God, not a result of works." †Ephesians 2:8, 9

GOD'S PARDON FOR GUILTY SINNERS is granted through faith alone in the Righteousness of Christ alone. It is the core of the gospel. It is fundamental.

It is foundational. "If this article stands the church stands," said Martin Luther. "If it falls the church falls." To the Reformer, John Calvin, faith is "…the hinge upon which everything turns."

It can be no other way, says Scripture. The necessary righteousness of man is a righteousness that comes from outside man. It is a righteousness transferred over to man. It is the righteousness of Christ Jesus. Man's only hope of justification before a holy God is the merit of Jesus Christ. Take this away, and man's faith is worthless. It is not worth the proverbial "hill of beans." Everything necessary to meet God's required standard of perfect righteousness—everything necessary to satisfy divine justice—has been fulfilled perfectly by the Savior. It is all about Jesus. All about what He has done. All about what He transfers to sinful man.

> *The necessary righteousness of man is a righteousness that comes from outside man. It is a righteousness transferred over to man. It is the Righteousness of Christ Jesus.*

The true story is told of how Arturo Toscanini had just conducted an electrifying rendition of Beethoven's Symphony Number 9. The audience applauded wildly. Toscanini bowed, and bowed, and bowed again. He then turned to the orchestra, "Gentlemen,

I am nothing. You are nothing. Beethoven is everything. Everything. Everything."

So it is with Jesus and our justification before God. It is all about the Savior! It is all about what He accomplished on behalf of guilty sinners. It is not about anything we have done.

> Nothing in my hand I bring
> > Simply to Thy cross I cling.
> Naked, come to Thee for grace
> > Foul, I to the fountain fly
> Wash me, Savior, or I die!
>
> —Augustus Toplady

Truly, it is all about faith. But even here, the Christian must take care. The believer's faith does not provide the ultimate grounds of salvation. The ultimate grounds of justification can only be the finished work of Jesus on the cross. The faith demanded by a holy God serves solely as the *means* of appropriating the justification that is in Christ Jesus.

> *The believer's faith does not provide the ultimate grounds of salvation. The ultimate grounds of justification can only be the finished work of Jesus Christ on the cross.*

The Savior is the valid object of the believer's saving faith. He is the indispensable one. Why? Because faith is only as good as its object. A small boy was asked by a scientific team to be lowered down the side of a cliff to recover some important specimens. The boy said *no*, even though the scientists offered to pay him a large sum of money. After continued efforts to persuade the boy, he finally consented. But he agreed only upon one condition: his father would have to be the one to hold the rope by which he would be lowered.

Those justified by a holy God are those rescued "...by faith in the Son of God who loved us and gave himself for us" (Galatians 2:20).

Justifying faith, therefore, is man's utter dependence on the saving grace of God that is in Christ Jesus.

Justification Is About Faith Alone But Not A Faith That Stands Alone

With the heart one believes and is justified. †Romans 10:10

You were washed, you were sanctified, you were justified, in the name of the Lord Jesus Christ and by the spirit of our God. †I Corinthians 6:11

He gave himself for us that we should no longer live for ourselves. †Galatians 1:4

A person is justified by works and not by faith alone. †James 2:24

SCRIPTURE REPEATEDLY EMPHASIZES THIS TRUTH: a faith that truly saves is never a faith that stands alone. It is a Holy Spirit given faith. It is anchored in the living God of holiness. It changes lives. "You were washed," says the apostle, of pride and contrary conduct (I Corinthians 6:11). Jesus becomes the object and the delight of transformed affections.

> A faith that truly saves is never a faith that stands alone.

Saving faith changes lives. It is not the consequence of people's imagination. It does not have its source, says Scripture, in people's minds. It springs from their hearts. "With the heart one believes and is justified," says Romans 10:10. It is just such a reality that has given birth to the popular proverb: "When God measures a man, He puts a tape around his heart, not his head."

Holy Spirit given faith is anchored in the living God of holiness. It is expressed in loving this God. Pleasing this God. Serving this God. Saving faith not only justifies; it sanctifies (I Corinthians 6:11). "Old things pass away. Behold, all things become new" (II Corinthians 5:17).

> *True justification is by faith alone. But never is justification by a faith that stands alone.*

Sanctifying change is certain. It also will take the rest of a person's life to complete. There will be struggles all the way. There can be no doubt about that. Those professing faith in Christ must be warned: the notion of a justified person remaining "carnal" in his conduct is a tragic heresy. True justification is by faith alone. But never is justification by a faith that stands alone. The hymn writer Isaac Watts had it right: "Love so amazing, so divine demands my soul, my life, my all."

Concluding Commentary

And about the ninth hour Jesus cried out with a loud voice... 'My God, My God, why have you forsaken me?'... Jesus cried out again with a loud voice and yielded up his spirit and behold, the curtain of the temple was torn in two, from top to bottom. And the earth shook, and the rocks were split. †Matthew 27:46-51

> *Jesus became the most filthy object ever set before God who cannot even look upon sin.*

IN READING THOSE WORDS, REDEEMED sons and daughters who love the Savior cannot help but be overwhelmed. They are forced to catch their breath. It is more than finite, sinful man can comprehend. Jesus is sacrificed upon Calvary's altar. Heaven's altar. The sinless Son of God endures the dreadful wrath of God's justice and judgment on sin.

There simply is no way in which the totality of what took place can ever be comprehended by sinful man. Jesus became the most filthy object ever set before God who cannot even look upon sin. It is incomprehensible! The Son of God experienced the agony of what it means to be *forsaken* by the Father. He became utterly repugnant to the Father. And He did it so that those He loves might *never* be forsaken by God.

It is staggering! Yet, there can be no other way for guilty man to be justified. Sin must be punished. The exacting of God's justice must be accomplished. But, praise God, the richness of God's saving grace must also be amazingly glorified. "For our sake, God made Jesus to be sin who knew no sin, so that in him, we might become the righteousness of God" (II Corinthians 5:20).

The ground of justification is, and must always be, the merit of Jesus Christ alone. It is a righteousness that God's amazing grace *imputes* to penitent believers. It also is the very reason why they excitedly sing:

> Let us join with the angel voices,
>> Let us join their happy song.
> All of heaven and earth rejoices
>> For the Lamb of God has come.
> He has come to rescue sinners,
>> Come to meet our desperate need.
> He was born to bring forgiveness,
>> Born for Calvary.
> Alleluia, Hope has come
>> Alleluia, Christ has come.
>
> —**Stephen Aitrogge**

"Works! Works! A man gets to heaven by works! I would as soon think of climbing to the moon on a rope of sand."

FOOD FOR THOUGHT

"Salvation is not in any sense God's response to anything in us. It is not something that we in any sense deserve or merit... The whole glory of salvation is that though we deserve nothing but punishment and hell and banishment out of the sight of God to all eternity, yet God, of His own love and grace and wondrous mercy, has granted us this salvation." QUOTES 26

"Justification does not mean... we are made righteous, but rather that God regards us as righteous and declares us to be righteous... Justification makes no actual changes in us. It is not something that results from what we do but rather something that is done for us. We have only been made righteous in the sense that God regards us righteous and pronounces us to be righteous." QUOTES #27

QUESTIONS FOR FEEDBACK

1 Why should the believer thank God every day that salvation is by grace alone?

2 Salvation that is a consequence of man's good deeds has always been a popular persuasion with the vast majority of people. How would you persuade someone that it is wrong?

3 What does the term "imputation" mean? What does the term "double imputation" mean?

4 Why must the obedience of Christ be the sole ground of our justification?

5 Are we really saved by faith that is alone?

6 What does "reconciliation" mean?

CHAPTER 11

GOING THE DISTANCE

"God does not stop at justifying us. He immediately begins in us the process of change called sanctification. Justification freed us from the guilt of sin and its condemnation. The process of sanctification begins to free us from the power of sin and its rule in our life... The evidence that someone is saved is that his life is being changed." **QUOTES #28**

Sanctification Takes Perseverance

IN THE WORLD OF ENTERTAINMENT the expression *going the distance* has become a familiar idiom. For example, the theme song for Disney's animated film *Hercules* is titled "Go the Distance." Not too long ago Hollywood also produced a romantic comedy about a long distance love affair worth fighting for. Once more, the caption of this film was "Going the Distance." But the expression is probably best remembered from the Academy Award winning story "Rocky."

Rocky Balboa, the "Italian Stallion" is an unknown boxer from Philadelphia. He is about to capitalize on a once in a lifetime opportunity of going into the ring with Apollo Creed, the world heavy weight boxing champion. Apollo Creed is the colorful undefeated pugilist known in the boxing world as "The Master of Disaster," "The King of Sting," "The Count of Monty Fisto."

So why does this reigning heavyweight champion of the world choose to fight a virtually unknown brawler from the projects? The "champ" explains his decision to fight Rocky Balboa this way: "Who discovered America? An Italian; right? What better way to celebrate its 200th birthday, than to 'get it on' with one of his descendants?" He then quickly boasts that he will knock out Rocky Balboa in three rounds!

The challenger's friends are understandably brutally frank in their pronouncements. "Apollo Creed will make hamburger out of Rocky." The ambitious pugilist listens to every word. Not surprisingly, he is well aware of the fact that the odds are overwhelmingly against his ever winning this fight. But regardless, he's going to accept the challenge. He tells his friends why. "Nobody's ever *gone the distance* with Creed. And if I can go that distance, you see, and that bell rings and I'm still standin,' I'm gonna know for the first time in my life, see, that I weren't just another bum from the neighborhood."

The movie has become one of Hollywood's most financially successful films. Some even have described it as a "cult classic."

I open this chapter with comments about Rocky because there are parallels in that movie to the spiritual discipline of sanctification. The Apostle Paul puts it this way: "But as for you, O man of God, flee these things (love of money, etc.). Pursue righteousness, godliness, faith, love steadfastness, gentleness. *fight the good fight of faith*" (I Timothy 6:11, 12).

God's servant is saying that it takes determination and perseverance to *go the distance*. And so, to motivate his colleague in ministry, Paul says, "I charge you in the presence of God... *fight the good fight of faith... take hold* of the eternal life to which you were called."

The Apostle Peter says much the same thing. Because he also recognizes the intense nature of this life-long spiritual struggle, he writes: "Prepare your minds *for battle*. Be sober minded... as obedient children, do not be conformed to the passions of your former ignorance, but as He who called you is holy, you also be holy in all your conduct" (I Peter 1:13-15). Peter is saying, dig in! Resist! Prepare for sustained exertion! Why? Once more, it is because it takes determination to *go the distance*.

Sanctification: Its Biblical Meaning

Strive for holiness without which no one will see the Lord. †Hebrews 12:14

Whoever says he abides in Christ, ought to walk in the same way in which He walked. †John 2:6

THE BIBLICAL EXPRESSION "SANCTIFICATION" SIMPLY means "to be set apart". Throughout Scripture, God sets apart people. He sets apart places. He also sets apart things. And God does this in order that His purposes may be accomplished. "Before I formed you in the womb," says God of His servant Jeremiah, "I knew you; before you were born I sanctified you; and I ordained you a prophet to the nations" (Jeremiah 1:5).

In the book of Exodus God sets apart a specific place for His purposes. He sanctifies the tabernacle in the wilderness as a place of worship. "There will I meet with the children of Israel and the tabernacle shall be sanctified by my glory" (Exodus 29:43).

In Genesis, God sets apart the seventh day of the week as a holy day of rest. "God blessed the seventh day and sanctified it because in it He rested from all his work" (Genesis 2:2, 3).

In an incomparable way, the writer of Hebrews emphasizes that when an individual is sanctified today, that person is being "set apart" to carry out the purpose of God. "For by one offering He (Jesus) has perfected forever those who are being sanctified" (Hebrews 10:14).

> The biblical expression "sanctification" simply means "to be set apart."

Sanctification points to the fact that true saving faith is not just a *personal* faith. It also is a *practical* faith. It is a *life-changing* faith. With respect to progressive sanctification, it is a faith in which the believer is enabled, through the indwelling person of the Holy Spirit, "...more and more to die unto sin and to live unto righteousness" (I Peter 2:24).

Sanctification and the Sanctifier

That the offering of the Gentiles might be acceptable, sanctified by the Holy Spirit. †**Romans 15:16**

God from the beginning chose you for salvation through sanctification by the Holy Spirit and belief in the truth. †**I Thessalonians 2:13**

...to those who are elect... according to the foreknowledge of God the Father, in the sanctification of the Spirit, for obedience to Jesus Christ.
†**I Peter 1:1, 2**

SANCTIFICATION DEMANDS THE ENABLING POWER of the Holy Spirit. As long as we think we can save ourselves by our own determination, we only make the evil that is within us stronger than ever. But with the empowering of the Holy Spirit everything changes. In fact, every time a Christian stands to recite the Apostles' Creed, declaring "...I believe in the Holy Spirit," that person is saying something exceedingly important. They not only are professing their faith in a living God, they also are affirming that this very God, in the person of the Holy Spirit, is willing to enter individual lives and change these lives.

> As long as we think we can save ourselves by our own determination, we only make the evil that is within us stronger than ever.

How does it happen? The answer is this: it happens in the same way in which believers experience the early blessings of justification.

It happens by faith alone. In the words of Colossians 2:6, 7, "As you have *received* Christ Jesus the Lord, so *walk* in Him." In other words, the gospel of God's grace that saves is the same gospel of grace that sanctifies.

> The gospel of God's grace that saves is the same gospel of grace that sanctifies.

That's an important principle. Why? Because the believer who attempts to achieve sanctification by the sheer willpower of the flesh soon will discover he has entered into a roller coaster ride of ups and downs. He has entered a path on which he will experience both hollow victories and harmful failures.

However, what is also true is this: progressive sanctification demands determination. It is why repeatedly in Scripture, the Christian is told to strive for holiness without which no one shall see the Lord. At the same time, the business of striving to "will" and to "work" cannot be carried out without the enabling of the Holy Spirit. The message of Philippians 3:12, 13 is one saying that the Christian's "will" and Christian's "work" become the arenas in which this all-powerful presence of the Holy Spirit perfects the very ministry that will bring about "God's good pleasure."

> *The Holy Spirit begins with the mind, because if this transforming ministry does not start with the mind, never will it happen in the heart.*

How is this sanctifying work accomplished? The message of Romans 12:2 says, the Holy Spirit works through the believer's mind. The apostle writes, "Do not be conformed to this world, but be transformed by the renewal of your mind, that by testing you may discern what is the will of God, what is good and acceptable and perfect."

The Holy Spirit begins with the mind, because if this transforming ministry does not start with the mind, never will it happen in the heart. And if it does not impact the heart, neither will it happen in a person's daily walk. It is this intimate experience of the Holy Spirit, working through the Word, and working within the minds and hearts of God's people that both equips and enables God's transforming ministry to move forward. When believers are walking in the light of God's Word, the Holy Spirit empowers them not to "...gratify the desires of the flesh" (Galatians 5:16). The Holy Spirit enables them to shine as lights in the world.

Sanctification: What it Means to Live Out Practical Holiness

I esteem all your precepts concerning all things to be right and I hate every false way. †Psalm 119:128

Whatever you do, work heartily, as for the Lord and not for man... You are serving the Lord Christ. †Colossians 3:23, 24

> He that says he abides in Christ, ought himself also to walk, even as He walked. †1 John 2:6

PRACTICAL HOLINESS IS JUST THAT. It is exceedingly pragmatic. It impacts attitudes and actions. It involves hating what God hates. It involves loving what God loves. It involves measuring one's life by the standard of God's Word. It involves striving to become "...conformed to the image of Jesus"(Romans 8:29).

Practical holiness is esteeming others better than one's self. It is understanding what Abraham felt when he said, "I am but dust and ashes" (Genesis 18:27). It is understanding the sentiment of Jacob when he said, "I am less than the least of all your mercies" (Genesis 32:10). It is understanding the brokenness of Paul when he wrote, "I am the chief of sinners" (I Timothy 1:15). It is never to be at peace with sin. To mourn over sin. To long to be free from sin.

Practical holiness glorifies God because it incorporates a spirit of mercy and benevolence toward others. It is loving others more than one's own comfort, more than one's own convenience. It is not being content to stand by, simply doing no harm. It is following a path in which self is denied in order to minister to others. It is to be like Dorcas,"... full of good works and alms deeds" (Acts 9:36).

"The reigning cliché of the day," according to TV commentator Charles Krauthammer, "is that in order to love others one must first learn to love one's self." This formulation, he accurately wrote, is simply "a license for unremitting self-indulgence, because the quest for self-love is endless. By the time you have finally learned to love yourself, you'll find yourself playing golf at Leisure World." (TIME magazine, June 28, 1993).

Practical holiness is dramatically different from the kind of self-indulgent mindset described in Krauthammer's commentary. It involves people in consistent deeds of compassion. It is these very acts that do much to "...proclaim the excellencies of Him who has called us out of darkness and into His marvelous light" (I Peter 2:9).

Sanctification: A Continuing Process

...The flesh lusts against the Spirit, and the Spirit against the flesh; and these are contrary to one another, so that you do not do the things that you wish. †Galatians 5:17

If we say that we have no sin, we deceive ourselves, and the truth is not in us. †I John 1:8

IN WRITING TO TIMOTHY, THE apostle Paul clearly understood the paradoxical and paralyzing power of sin's presence in a believer's life. It is what compelled him to write: "Christ Jesus came into the world to save sinners, of whom I am foremost" (I Timothy 1:15). His confession was not simply an indulgence in emotional hyperbole. This man was saying, the more like Jesus, he became, the more *unlike* Jesus he realized he was.

He also was a man who knew that preventing sin and producing spiritual growth is never easy. In writing to believers in Rome, he puts it this way: "I have the desire to do what is right, but not the ability to carry it out... I do not do the good I want but the evil I do not want is what I keep on doing" (Romans 7:18, 19).

God's servant is describing a profound conflict that every Christian experiences. In fact, if he lived today and if he watched the movie "Rocky," he would say the pugilist was absolutely right! It always takes more than we ever expect "to go the distance."

St. Augustine also reminds us why this is so. "Before we were justified, there was only one rider on our horse and he was the devil." But after justification, everything has changed. "Now," said Augustine, "there are two riders and they are fighting for the same horse."

Little wonder, therefore, that the apostle writes, "Who will deliver us?" (Romans 7:24). It's a simple question, but it is not a cry of despair. Paul feels no sense of hopelessness. He is a man who most certainly knows the answer to his question. He spells it out in the very next verse: "Thanks be to God," this deliverance all God's people need to experience is one that comes "through Jesus Christ our Lord" (Romans 7:25). He is the one who, through the ministry of the Holy Spirit, enables His followers to go the distance.

> *In writing to Timothy, the apostle Paul clearly understood the paradoxical and paralyzing power of sin's presence in a believer's life.*

He is the one who empowers God's people to live their lives in a circumspect manner. He fortifies His followers to do what Peter commands: "Be sober minded, be watchful. Your adversary the devil prowls around like a roaring lion, seeking someone to devour. Resist him, stand firm in your faith..." (I Peter 5:8, 9).

It takes vigilance to live the Christian life. Those who have seen the movie ROCKY will remember that overconfidence was one of Apollo Creed's flaws. Here was a man who underestimated Rocky Balboa, until in the very first round of their first fight, for the first time in the champion's life, Rocky Balboa had knocked him to the canvas.

Overconfidence is dangerous. An unknown commentator put it this way: "By our attitudes and actions we are writing, with a kind of invisible ink, our life's story. What a tragedy, that we scribble the pages so quickly and carelessly. We forget what I have written, I have written.—And what I have written, one day I must read."

FOOD FOR THOUGHT

"True faith is not passive but active. It requires that we meet certain conditions, that we allow the teachings of Christ to dominate our total lives from the moment we believe. The man of saving faith must be willing to be different from others. The effort to enjoy the benefits of redemption while enmeshed in the world is futile. We must choose one or the other; and faith quickly makes its choice, one from which there is no retreat." **QUOTES #29**

QUESTIONS FOR FEEDBACK

1. What is the relationship between man's work and God's work in sanctification?

2. What are the means (provisions) provided by God for the Christian's sanctification?

3. What does Philippians 2:12, 13 mean when it tells the Christian to "work out your salvation"? Is salvation dependent on our works?

4. From Romans 5:15-19, list what is true of an individual "in Adam," and an individual "in Christ."

5. According to I John 1:5-10, what are the pitfalls of denying the sin within us?

6. What does it mean that Christians are "the dwelling place of God"?

GOING THE DISTANCE

CHAPTER 12

MARATHONS ARE NOT FOR WIMPS

"The Holy Spirit never enters a man and then lets him live
just like the world that God hates..." **Quotes #30**

"...the criterion of true discipleship is continuance in Jesus' words...
The test of a true faith is perseverance in true piety to the end....
Where that godly walk in true piety is not forthcoming,
no professing Christian has the right to assume that he
is in fact a Christian." **Quotes #31**

True Believers Are in a Marathon

THE BIBLE OFTEN USES ANOTHER analogy—that of a long-distance running event, to highlight the single-minded perseverance required to win in the believer's "race of life." It is because long distance running requires serious self discipline, motivation, and sacrifice.

Long distance running will push a person to the limits. With this in mind, the writer of Hebrews challenges believers to "...*Run* with endurance the race that is set before us" (Hebrews 12:1).

Marathoners push themselves to the limit because they are determined to fulfill a dream they have trained months to accomplish. The rigors of preparing for this race have not been easy. Throughout training, there have been ups and downs, but the prize is worth the discipline. It is worth the perseverance.

On the day of the race as each runner approaches the starting line, they are focused. They have a goal. They are filled with visions of success. When the gun goes off, they are ready. But for many of these runners, about halfway through the race, pushing to that finish line doesn't seem to be a real option. Muscles are "spent." Everything within screams, "Stop!"

The best Marathoners, however, will rise to the challenge. Somehow, they will persevere! After their body cries, "stop," they will keep pushing on. After the mind wants to give up, they will endure. When they do persist, most will discover an inexplicable experience propelling them toward success. It's often described as a "second wind." Once more, the adrenaline kicks in. They enjoy a fresh burst of energy.

It is the kind of spiritual experience envisioned when believers are challenged to "...run with endurance the race that is set before us, looking to Jesus the founder and perfecter of our faith" (Hebrews 12:1). Such perseverance eventually pays rich dividends.

In the case of long distance runners, it enables them to cross the finish line. For those standing at the completion of a 26 mile marathon, it can be an unforgettable experience. Each participant crossing that finish line has a look of utter exhaustion on his face. Each also has an expression of unbelievable relief and triumph on his face.

The evidence of true saving faith, said Jesus, is perseverance

Bodies are aching. There is nothing more to give. But most importantly, these marathoners have achieved a monumental goal. Feelings of accomplishment are euphoric.

It is the agony and ecstasy of a similar perseverance that is envisioned in I Corinthians 9. "Do you not know that in a race all the runners compete, but only one receives the prize? So, run that you may obtain it." The race is never easy! Jesus never said it would be. But like that old gospel chorus says, "It will be worth it all when we see Jesus. One look from His dear face, all sorrows shall erase. So gladly run the race 'till we see Him."

The evidence of a true saving faith, said Jesus, is *perseverance*. It is those who "...persevere to the end" that are saved. Jesus was clear about that. He knew, those who follow Him will not find it is always a joyful experience. "You will be hated by all for my sake," said Jesus.

True Believers Can Neither Totally Nor Finally Fall Away

I will make an everlasting covenant with them that I will not turn away from them, to do them good; and I will put the fear of me in their hearts, so that they will not turn away from me. † Jeremiah 32:40

All that the Father gives me will come to me, and whoever comes to me, I will never cast out... and this is the will of him who sent me, that I should lose nothing of all that He has given me, but raise it up on the last day. † John 6:37-39

I am sure of this, that He who began a good work in you will bring it to completion at the day of Jesus Christ. ✝ **Philippians 1:6**

...may your spirit and soul and body be preserved complete, without blame at the coming of our Lord Jesus Christ. Faithful is He who calls you, and He also will bring it to pass. ✝ **I Thessalonians 5:23-24**

For I know whom I have believed, and I am convinced that He is able to guard until that day what has been entrusted to me. ✝ **II Timothy 1:12**

ENDURANCE FOR THE "TRUE BELIEVER" is a certainty. In days past, they have been justified by grace through faith. In days present, they are being sanctified by grace through faith. In days yet to come, they will be glorified by this same grace of God, through faith in the finished work of Christ their Savior. They can neither totally nor finally miss out on any stage of the God-ordained process involved in their salvation.

> *Endurance for the true believer is a certainty.*

It is all because of this: the steadfast love of God for His called out people is not based upon any unforeseen merit or righteousness in them. God's saving grace is anchored in His covenantal loving-kindness. As such, it is a loyal love. It will not change.

Amazed and humbled, God's servant writes, "See what kind of love the Father has given us, that we should be called children of God" (I John 3:1). The apostle stands in astonishment. God's love is unprecedented. It is "other-worldly." It will never let its object go.

> *God's saving grace is anchored in His covenantal lovingkindness. As such, it is a loyal love. It will not change.*

Looking down upon those who have "fled to Jesus," God in heaven does not have a "Plan B." All those whom God has called "...to His eternal glory in Christ," writes Peter, God also "...will himself restore, confirm, strengthen, and establish" (I Peter 5:10). In

Christ Jesus, they are utterly secure. The Puritan writer, Richard Baxter, put it this way, "In our first paradise in Eden there was a way to go out but no way to go in again. But as for the heavenly paradise, there is a way to go in, but not a way to go out."

True Believers May Fall into Grievous Sin

'Return, o faithless sons; I will heal your faithlessness.' 'Behold, we come to you, for you are the Lord our God.' †Jeremiah 3:22

I will heal their apostasy; I will love them freely, for my anger has turned from them. †Hosea 14:4

If we say we have no sin, we deceive ourselves, and the truth is not in us. If we confess our sins, he is faithful and just to forgive us our sins and to cleanse us from all unrighteousness. †I John 1:8, 9

IN SPITE OF THE FACT that the Scriptures repeatedly speak of the believer's "Eternal Security," many of God's people continue to find it to be a difficult teaching to embrace. They have had first-hand experience with those who at one time have displayed an enthusiastic profession of faith in the Savior. These same people now have drifted away from what they once professed. They have repudiated what they once professed to believe.

In every case it actually comes as no surprise to the Savior. Jesus predicted it would happen. Because a person verbalizes a profession of faith is no guarantee he truly possesses saving faith. Why is that? It is because people all too often "mask" what they truly believe.

I John 2:19 speaks of this reality. It broke the apostle's heart. He describes individuals who "...went out from us, but they were not really of us; for if they had been of us, they would have

Because a person verbalizes a profession of faith is no guarantee he truly possesses saving faith.

remained with us; but they went out, in order that it might be shown that they all are not of us."

The apostle John is writing about people who were known and loved in the local assembly of believers. He affirms that the reason they left was to show they were not of us. His emphasis is clear: those who are not true believers will leave. The true will stay.

Always, the evidence of true salvation is *perseverance*. It is why Peter writes, "...Brothers, be all the more diligent to make your calling and election sure, for if you practice these qualities you will never fall" (II Peter 1:10).

Those are words that emphasize the necessary Christian virtue of tenacity. Peter is painting a picture of patient perseverance. It also is why Jesus warned, "...He who stands firm to the end will be saved." He was not saying salvation is the reward for endurance. Rather, Jesus was teaching that endurance is the "hallmark" of those who are truly saved.

At the same time, it should never be assumed that once a person is born again, they never will "backslide." What we discover in life is this: such a sad experience usually is a gradual "drifting away." It is a gradual coasting downhill. It also should come as no surprise. If it were to happen suddenly, much like a splash of cold water in the face on a hot day, people would recognize it for what it is. Backsliding doesn't happen that way because Satan is sly. His tactics are subtle. What he brings about in a believer's life can be nearly imperceptible. All it takes is "...a little sleep, a little slumber, a little folding of the hands to rest" (Proverbs 8:10; 24:33).

We see it happening throughout redemptive history. Always there have been those who at one time seemed to love Jesus, only to later turn their backs on the Savior. Even some of those who followed Jesus in His earthly ministry "...went back and walked no more with Him."

What is also true is this: there always have been those who fell away but later returned. In John 20, Thomas had his moment of unbelief. Moses is another who demonstrated skeptical unbelief. David too, was a man who sinned grievously. Peter also knew firsthand about this sad reality of denial. But each of these men also demonstrated that complete restoration most assuredly is possible.

The God of the gospel message is merciful. He is ever ready to forgive. He is "...ready to forgive, gracious and merciful, slow to anger and abounding in steadfast love" (Nehemiah 9:17). He never will abandon His own.

> *The God of the gospel message is merciful. He is ever ready to forgive.*

At times He may use extreme measures to bring His people back. But God does bring them out of their darkness.

The Psalmist describes how "...they cried to the Lord in their trouble, and He delivered them from their distress." He then writes, "...Let them thank the Lord for His steadfast love for His wondrous works to the children of men" (Psalm 107:10-15).

So how does this backsliding happen? In the Upper Room Jesus tells us how it happens. Knowing Peter would deny Him in just a few hours, Jesus says, "Simon! Simon! Indeed Satan has asked for you that he may sift you as wheat." What a blunt commentary that is! Jesus is telling Peter, You are "a piece of cake" in the hands of Satan. In fact, Peter, it won't be long before you crumble like a dry old piece of cake.

Yet here's the encouraging news, not just for Peter but also for every one of us. "...I have prayed for you, that your faith should not fail," said Jesus. "And *when* you have returned to me, strengthen your brethren." In those words of Jesus is encapsulated the very reason for Peter's perseverance and for ours. It is not a case of "if" you return, said Jesus. It is a matter of "when" you return!

The Perseverance of the True Believer is Tied To the Intercession of the Savior

I have manifested your name to the people whom you gave to me out of the world. Yours they are, and you gave them to me... I am praying for them... for those whom you have given me, for they are yours... Keep them from the evil one... Sanctify them in the truth, your word is truth. †John 17:6, 9, 15, 17

FREQUENTLY, BELIEVERS WILL REJOICE IN the fact that Jesus is the Father's gift to them. And He is! But an equally amazing fact is highlighted in the High Priestly Prayer of Jesus. No less than seven times in this prayer, Jesus affirms that born-again believers are the Father's "love gift" to the Son. That's a staggering statement. It also highlights a relevant question: Would the Father present to His Son a gift that would simply fade away? Never!

> *Jesus affirms that born again believers are the Father's "love gift" to the Son.*

In spite of failures and faults, sinners are saved by God's grace. God even affirms, "I am glorified in them." That's amazing! It is an important dimension of God's incredible mercy to a wicked people. It is why the Puritan, John Cotton, wrote: "It may be that we are sinful; but God did not love us for our goodness, and neither will He cast us off for our wickedness."

Peter, clearly the leader of our Lord's "apostolic band" is "Exhibit A." He is weak. Impetuous. Erratic. Cowardly. Hotheaded. He fails miserably and he fails often. But was his faith snuffed out because of cowardly denials? Never! It did not happen for the most encouraging of reasons: Jesus was praying for Peter. Such prayers of Jesus never go unanswered.

> *God did not love us for our goodness, and neither will He cast us off for our wickedness.*

As 21st century believers, we need to learn a most important lesson from this fact. Left to ourselves, we are all capable of a radical falling away from the Lord. Yet, Jesus said, "I do not pray for these alone, but also for those who will believe in me, through their word" (John 17:20). What a monumental blessing that is. It is a truth that impacted the author of Hebrews. It is why he wrote: "He is able to save forever those who draw near to God through Him, since He always lives to make intercession for them." (Hebrews 7:25). What a bold certainty that is!

It is a truth that also humbled a man like John Wesley. It is why he penned this moving anthem of praise to God's grace:

> He ever lives above,
> > For me to intercede,
> His all-redeeming love
> > His precious blood to plead;
> His blood atoned for every race,
> > His blood atoned for every race,
> And sprinkles now the throne of grace.
> > Five bleeding wounds He bears,
> Received on Calvary;
> > They pour effectual prayers,
> They strongly plead for me;
> > Forgive him, O forgive, they cry,
> Forgive him, O forgive, they cry,
> > Nor let that ransomed sinner die.

The True Believer's Perseverance is a Work of the Holy Spirit

In him we have obtained an inheritance, having been predestined according to the purpose of Him who works all things according to the counsel of his will... In Him you also when you heard the word of truth, the gospel of your salvation, and believed in Him, were sealed with the promised Holy Spirit, who is the guarantee of our inheritance until we acquire possession of it, to the praise of His glory. †**Ephesians 1:11-14**

BELIEVERS ARE ETERNALLY SECURE BECAUSE of the High Priestly ministry of Jesus. They also are secure because they have been "...sealed with the promised Holy Spirit who is the guarantee of (their) inheritance until (they) acquire possession of it, to the praise of His glory" (Ephesians 1:14).

In the ancient world when a king issued an edict, the seal made by the sovereign's signet ring was a pledge: what was declared, would be carried out! In a somewhat similar fashion, the message of Ephesians 1:11-14 affirms that the indwelling Holy Spirit is God's seal of ownership of the believer's life. The Holy Spirit's all-powerful presence becomes a pledge from God. What has been promised most assuredly will be performed.

> *The Holy Spirit's all-powerful presence becomes a pledge from God. What has been promised most assuredly will be performed.*

The trucking industry has a practice that at least in a limited way illustrates this sealing by the Holy Spirit. When a truck is fully loaded with certain cargo, and ready for its run, a plastic seal is many times affixed around the lock on the cargo door. This seal cannot be broken before the truck reaches its destination without the penalty of loss of one's job.

Neither can the sealing of the Holy Spirit in a believer's life be broken before that individual reaches the heavenly destination God is preparing for him. It is why Samuel Chadwick highlights the fact that the Holy Spirit endues men with divine authority and power. He affirms, "The Holy Spirit does not come upon methods, but men." He writes, "He does not work through organizations, but through men. He does not dwell in buildings, but in men."

The True Believer's Perseverance and God's Message in I Peter 1:3-9

Blessed be the God and Father of our Lord Jesus Christ! According to His great mercy, He has caused us to be born again to a living hope... to an inheritance that is imperishable... kept in heaven for you, who by God's power are being guarded through faith for salvation ready to be revealed in the last times. In this you rejoice, though now for a little while... you have been grieved by various trials, so that the tested genuineness of your faith... may be found to result in praise and glory and honor at the revelation of Jesus Christ. Though you have not seen Him, you love Him... obtaining the outcome of your faith, the salvation of your souls. †I Peter 1:3-9

THE APOSTLE PETER OPENS HIS first epistle with this weighty word of assurance. He affirms, that God does not stand back after He has caused believers to be born again. Rather, God uses His omnipotent power to protect them all through life for this great salvation that is ready to be revealed to them. Because of this, they are profoundly secure in Him. First, the apostle writes, they are "...born again to a living hope." Human hopes and dreams inevitably fade and ultimately disappoint. But the believer's hope in Jesus Christ cannot die. It is a hope that is "both sure and steadfast" says Hebrews 6:19. It

The power that keeps the believer secure in Jesus Christ is a sovereign power. It is an omnipotent power. An omniscient power.

will come to complete fulfillment. It will not die. It will be an eternal fulfillment. It is "...reserved in heaven."

The power that keeps the believer secure in Christ Jesus is a sovereign power. It is an omnipotent power. An omniscient power. Even now, says God's servant, believers are "...protected by the power of God through faith for a salvation ready to be revealed in the last times." Throughout their days, they are sustained by the never failing grace and power of God.

> *Pain in this life is the very experience that perfects the purposes of God.*

Paradoxical as it may seem, from God's perspective, says Peter, pain in this life is the very experience that perfects the purposes of God. Faith is fortified through distressing times in life. It may catch God's people by surprise, says Peter, but the "fiery trials" of life are "...obtaining the outcome of (their) faith, the salvation of (their) souls" (I Peter 1:7-9).

"Though you have not seen Him you love Him, and though you do not see Him now, but believe in Him, you greatly rejoice with joy inexpressible and full of glory" (I Peter 1:8). In those words, Peter most likely is demonstrating a heartfelt humility. He is commending suffering saints who never have even seen the Savior. Yet, though they have never seen Jesus, they have a deep love for Him. They have an utter trust in Him.

In all probability, Peter is reflecting on the fact that he was privileged to walk with Jesus and to listen to the teachings of Jesus. Even to look into the eyes of Jesus. Yet, he also had denied the Master. He had turned his back on the Savior. It is almost a certainty, that Peter never could forget how, after the resurrection, Jesus had come to him and questioned his love. Jesus questioned his love, not once, but three times. "Peter, do you love me?" (John 21:17).

It must have been a shattering experience! But Peter did repent and he was restored. This experience became a painful time of testing, out of which this man of God was purified. With such an encounter in mind, the apostle's words seem all the more poignant: "You've never seen Him, yet you love Him and you don't see Him now, yet you believe in Him." In all likelihood, when Peter writes those words of affirmation they come from a humble, chastened servant of the Savior. Among other things, his words are meant to motivate every redeemed child of God today.

It is this love for the Savior that becomes one of those undeniable assurances that a follower of Jesus will persevere to the end. Because of a fervent affection for the Savior they will long to promote His glory. They will long to worship Him, serve Him and be with Him.

> *It is love for the Savior that becomes one of those undeniable assurances that a follower of Jesus will persevere to the end.*

Such thinking moved the apostle John to write: "Beloved, we are God's children now, and what we will be has not yet appeared, but we know that when He appears we shall be like Him, because we shall see Him as He is. And everyone who thus hopes in Him purifies himself as He is pure" (I John 3:2-3).

True belivers will persevere to the end. At the same time, God's servant Jude also knew, that believers persevere only because their God graciously perseveres in them. It is this confidence that motivated Jude to write the following magnificent doxology, extolling God's tenacious never-failing grace:

> "Now to Him who is able to keep you from stumbling and to present you faultless before the presence of His glory with great joy, to the only God our Savior, through Jesus Christ our Lord, be glory, majesty, dominion, and authority, before all time and now and forever. Amen." †Jude 24-25

FOOD FOR THOUGHT

"To His own sheep, then, Jesus gives eternal life… The consequence of His knowing His sheep, and His gift of eternal life, is that they shall never perish… To think otherwise would entail the conclusion that Jesus had failed in the explicit assignment given Him by the Father, to preserve all those given to Him. The ultimate security of Jesus' sheep rests with the Good Shepherd." QUOTES #32

QUESTIONS FOR FEEDBACK

1. In John 10, Jesus said, no one can snatch his sheep out of his hand. What does "no one" mean? Is it possible that Jesus meant "no one" except ourselves? Did Jesus mean we can jump out of God's hand if we want to do so?

2. Does what is sometimes described as the "security of the believer," mean that salvation is certain if we have once believed, whether or not we continue to devote ourselves to growing in grace.

3. What claims does Jesus make in John 6:35-40?

4. Does the high priestly ministry of Jesus impact the perseverance of his people? What does Hebrews 9:11-15 teach about this?

5. What does the message of Philippians 1:6 teach us about security?

6. In II Peter 1:5, with everything given to us for our life in Christ, why does the apostle says we must "add to our faith"? Why is what the apostle writes in II Peter 1:5-11 so desirable for believers?

MARATHONS ARE NOT FOR WIMPS

QUOTES

1. Lewis Smedes, *Standing on the Promises*
   Thomas Nelson Publishers, p. 9

2. Edward Donnelly, *Peter*
   Banner of Truth Trust, p. 72

3. A. W Tozer, *The Knowledge of The Holy*
   Harper and Brothers Publishers, p 10

4. J. I. Packer, *Knowing Scripture*
   Inter Varsity Press, pp. 2-10

5. Arthur W. Pink, *The Divine Inspiration of the Bible*
   Baker Book House, p. 7

6. Alexander C. De Jong, *What I Confess*
   Baker Book House, p. 8

7. R. C. Sproul, *Essential Truths of the Christian Faith*
   Grayson Publishers, p 35

8. Stuart Olyott, *The Three Are One*
   Evangelical Press, p. 60

9. A. W. Tozer, *The Knowledge of The Holy*
   Harper and Brothers Publishers, p.1; p.79

10. Arthur W. Pink, *The Attributes of God*
    Baker Book House, p. 7

11. Robert L. Reymond
    A New Systematic Theology of the Christian Faith
    Thomas Nelson Publishers, p. 161

12. A. W. Tozer, *The Knowledge of The Holy*
    Harper and Brothers Pub., pp 60-61

13. A. W. Tozer, *The Knowledge of The Holy*
    Harper and Brothers Publishers, p. 104

14. Chip Ingram, *God As He Longs for You to See Him*
    Baker Book House, pp. 20-21

15. R. C. Sproul, *Essential Truths of the Christian Faith*
    Grayson Publishers, p.132

16. Bryan Chapell, *The Wonder of It All*
    Crossway Books, p.84

17. J. I. Packer, *God's Words*
    Inter Varsity Press, p. 167

18. Bryan Chapell, *The Wonder of It All*
    Crossway Books, pp. 54-55

19. John Murray, *The Covenant of Grace*
    Presbyterian and Reformed Publishing Co., p. 4

20. R. C. Sproul, *Truths We Confess*, (Vol. 1)
    P & R. Publishing, pp. 205, 214, 220

21. R.C. Sproul, *Truths We Confess*, (Vol. 2)
    P & R Publishing, p. 2

22. Robert L. Reymond
    A New Systematic Theology of the Christian Faith
    Thomas Nelson Publishers, pp. 343, 356

23. G. I. Williamson
    The Westminster Confession of Faith for Study Classes
    Presbyterian & Reformed Publishing Co., pp. 89-90

24. John Murray, *Redemption Accomplished and Applied*
    Banner of Truth, p. 103

25. James Montgomery Boice
    Foundations of the Christian Faith
    Inter Varsity Press, p. 329

26. D. M. Lloyd-Jones, *God's Way of Reconciliation*
    Evangelical Press, p. 130

27. D. M. Lloyd-Jones, *Romans 3*
    Banner of Truth Trust, p. 2

28. Peter Jeffery, *Bitesize Theology*
    Evangelical Press, pp. 81-82

29. A. W. Tozer, *Man the Dwelling Place of God*
    C P I Publishers, p. 61

30. A. W. Tozer, *When He Is Come*
    Send The Light Publishers, p. 49

31. Robert L. Reymond
    A New Systematic Theology of the Christian Faith
    Thomas Nelson Publishers, p. 794

32. D. A. Carson, *John*
    Inter Varsity Press, p. 393

CPSIA information can be obtained at www.ICGtesting.com
Printed in the USA
LVOW090246100212

267978LV00002BA/3/P